HART WOOD

Don Hibbard

Glenn Mason

Karen Weitze

HART WOOD

ARCHITECTURAL REGIONALISM IN HAWAII

A LATITUDE 20 BOOK

UNIVERSITY
of HAWAI'I
PRESS
HONOLULU

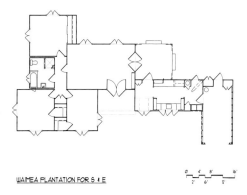

WAIMEA PLANTATION FOR S ₹ E

LIBRARY OF CONGRESS CATALOGING-IN-PUBLICATION DATA

Hibbard, Don.

  Hart Wood : architectural regionalism in Hawaii / Don
Hibbard, Glenn Mason, and Karen Weitze.

      p. cm.

  "A latitude 20 book."

  Includes bibliographical references and index.

  ISBN 978-0-8248-3236-0 (hardcover : alk. paper)

  1. Wood, Hart, 1880–1957—Criticism and interpretation. 2.
Regionalism in architecture—Hawaii. I. Mason, Glenn (Glenn
E.) II. Weitze, Karen J. III. Title.

  NA737.W515.A8 2010

  720.92—dc22

                              2009026865

University of Hawai'i Press books are printed on acid-free paper
and meet the guidelines for permanence and durability of the
Council on Library Resources.

Designed by Julie Matsuo-Chun

Printed by Thomson-Shore, Inc.

THIS BOOK IS DEDICATED TO OUR CHILDREN.

Conceived before any of them,

it waited until they had grown

before blossoming.

THE DICTIONARY defines an architect as a master builder, and architecture as the art or science of building. These definitions, however, take no account of architecture as a fine art. Yet it is so considered and accepted among the artistic fraternity. And as a fine art it is one of the most important of all the fine arts in the daily lives of all of us who live in civilized communities. The contemplation or enjoyment of any one of the others, such as music, painting, sculpture, poetry, etc., requires some expenditure of effort, time, or money and is for most of us a matter of casual or at least infrequent occurrence. Whereas architecture, in some form or another, good or bad, confronts us practically 24 hours of every day, and causes definite reactions on our conscious experience.

—HART WOOD

CONTENTS

ACKNOWLEDGMENTS

First and foremost we extend a debt of gratitude to Charles R. Sutton, Vladimir Ossipoff, and Robert Fox, the trustees of the Hart Wood Foundation, who so many years ago pointed us down the trail which has led to this book. Much belated thanks to Diane Miyakawa, Janine Shinoki Clifford, Patrick Seguirant, and Jerry Unabia, who continued the energy and information flowing through their student projects at the University of Hawaii. Grants received from the A & B Foundation and the Atherton Family Foundation are very much appreciated, as they provided the wherewithal not only to bring this project into printed form but to do so in a manner befitting the artistry of Hart Wood. *Mahalo* also to the gracious, helpful, and ever-friendly people at the University of Hawai'i Press, especially Masako Ikeda and Cheri Dunn, and to our copy editor, Lee Motteler, all of whom smoothly handled the publication process, contributing their knowledge and expertise to achieve a better book. A special *mahalo* to Julie Matsuo-Chun for so superbly applying her artistry to beautifully present the artistry of Hart Wood.

Over the decades many people have assisted us in our endeavor to try to understand Hart Wood and his work. We thank all of the home and building owners who allowed us access to their property and materials.

Mahalo also to Benton and Kenneth Wood for sharing their memories of their father, to Patty Wood for recollections of Hart Wood's later years, to Douglas Yanagihara, Paul Okumoto, and Ormand Kelley who provided information on the operation of Wood's office during their post–World War II tenure there, and to Justin Tomita for sharing the materials his father produced while working in Wood's office in the 1930s. We also appreciate the assistance rendered by Georgianna Contiguglia, Gail Fogerty, Darrell D. Garwood, Nancy K. Sherbert, Eleanor M. Gehres, Dr. Steven Jansen, George M. Keefer, Mrs. Miles, Sophia Kreling, Fred Lee and Thomas Plant, Mary Ann Thompson, the late Joseph Baird, and Tony Wren.

Our deep appreciation to the staffs at the Kansas State Historical Society; Denver Public Library; Colorado Historical Society; American Institute of Architects Archives in Washington, D.C.; Atascadero Historical Society; Bancroft Library and Environmental Design Library at the University of California, Berkeley; California State Library's Sacramento Branch; Douglas County Historical Society in Lawrence, Kansas; Hays Public Library; L.D.S. Genealogical Library in Carmichael, California; San Francisco Public Library; San Mateo County Recorder's Office; University City Library in St. Louis, Missouri; Hawaii State Archives; Bishop Museum; Hawaiian Historical Society; and Hawaii State Library who were, as always, very helpful and accommodating in their assistance. Finally, special thanks go out to friends, colleagues, and family for their encouragement and inquiries about the book they thought was finished years ago.

INTRODUCTION

Although today he is overshadowed by former partner Charles W.
Dickey, Hart Wood is one of the giants of Hawaii's regionalist design
movement and arguably its most creative advocate. The first architect in
Hawaii known to meld Asian and Western forms, some of his best buildings, such as the A and B Building and the Board of Water Supply Administration Building, remain icons of Hawaii's architectural legacy more
than fifty years after Wood's death in 1957.

This book traces the development of this remarkable talent from
his early upbringing in Kansas and Colorado through his early work in
California and from his coming to Hawaii as C. W. Dickey's partner in
1919 through his subsequent thirty-eight years in Hawaii. The book con-
siders his rich experiences in California, first as the chief draftsman for
the highly regarded beaux arts firm of Bliss and Faville and then as head
of his own office. This formative mainland period contributed heavily to
his sublime sense of line and color, as well as to his confident handling
of applied ornamentation. These years also reinforced within him a keen
awareness of architecture's relationship with the landscape. Armed with
these well-learned architectural lessons and inculcated with a spirit of
architectural regionalism from his years of practice in the San Francisco

Bay area, Wood arrived in Honolulu and quickly assumed a leadership position within Hawaii's small architectural community.

Enchanted by the vivid beauty of the Islands with their benevolent climate, exotic flora, and cosmopolitan culture, Wood almost immediately commenced a quest to architecturally embody the aura of Hawaii. The indelible mark left by his effort remains evident throughout the city in the magnificent and graceful buildings he designed.

Initially concentrating on forms, he eclectically blended architectural elements from Hawaii's missionary tradition with those of the mild-tempered Mediterranean. His work embraced the lanai as an outdoor living space, and he self-consciously utilized local materials such as coral block and lava rock in new and distinctive ways. The First Church of Christ Scientist on Punahou Street exquisitely summarizes Wood's initial encounter with and response to Hawaii.

Emerging as an avid advocate for appropriate regional design, Wood's impeccable aesthetic sensibility immersed him deeply within Hawaii's artistic community, which had Mrs. C. M. Cooke at its core. His design of her house on Makiki Heights (now the Contemporary Arts Center) in 1924 opened totally new realms of architectural exploration, as here East literally met West. Built as a house not only for Mrs. Cooke but also for her Asian art collection, the dwelling blended elements of China's building tradition with those of the West and Hawaii. This new avenue ultimately led to such commissions as the Chinese Christian Church on King Street and the S. and G. Gump Building in Waikiki. The latter—a commercial building that appeared more as a residence, with its landscaped gardens and grassy setbacks from the street—opened up the possibility for a building such as C. Brewer's corporate headquarters, designed by Bertram Goodhue's successor firm, Mayers, Murray and Phillip.

The melding of Asian and Western forms reached an apex with the construction of the Alexander & Baldwin Building on Bishop Street. This high point also signaled the demise of the partnership of Dickey and Wood. In the ensuing years, Wood reconceptualized his approach to regional design, moving beyond specific architectural forms to emphasize instead the underlying precepts that characterized the essence of Hawaii: simplicity, comfort, friendliness, and hospitality. He reintroduced the conscious rusticity of board and batten exterior walls, as in the Waimea Community Center on Kauai, and his house plans would assume a sprawling horizontality. In addition, he undertook the design of pumping stations for the Board of Water Supply, elevating the mundane into the ethereal realm of civic beauty.

The late 1930s brought the precepts of modern architecture to Hawaii. Wood approached the new direction with caution, counseling that architects needed to keep abreast of progress but at the same time should be mindful of Hawaii's rich heritage. The Honolulu Board of Water Supply's Administration Building on Beretania Street, designed in the late 1940s and completed shortly after Hart Wood's death in 1957, well adhered to this sage advice.

In the words of his former employer, W. B. Faville, Wood was "an Architect of marked ability, sterling character." This book emphasizes his ability, but the reader should keep in mind the sterling character and lofty ideals of the man as well. We three coauthors never experienced Hart Wood the person—and, as it turns out, few people did. However, a few people still remain who had encounters with him and remember his persona. Wood was in many ways an anachronism, with a stern personality rather reminiscent of the Puritan forefathers of the Island's first missionaries. His character was dominated by a practicality that moved him to give *The Prince and the Pauper* to Justin Tomita, the six-year-old son of his head draftsman, James Tomita. He had a lack of tact. Yet in every way he was a gentleman; a very reserved and private person. Consequently, it is the outer, oftentimes intimidating or brusque character of Hart Wood that many people remember: the paragon of integrity, seeker of perfection, strong willed, persistent, and insistent upon a quality handling of his project vision. Yet also within him resided an extremely sensitive, artistic soul, a quiet personality that blended into the woodwork. It was these qualities that intermingled in the man and allowed the works we see on the following pages to come forth.

Throughout his career Wood remained aware of architecture as an integral and edifying part of any community, thanks to its ability to convey the underlying convictions and spirit of a society. His work embodied the highest aspirations of the leaders of Hawaii during the first half of the twentieth century. Products of a gentler, more idealistic time, they stand today as continued reminders of an abiding excellence that is as vital today as it was yesterday.

INFLUENCES
OF YOUTH

1

Born in Philadelphia on December 26, 1880, Hart Wood was the son of Thomas Hart Benton Wood, the nephew of Louis M. H. Wood, and the grandson of Samuel Wood. The Woods were all active artisans in the building trades of the nineteenth and early-twentieth centuries.[1] By 1850, Samuel Wood (b. 1817, Virginia), a Scotch-Irishman descended from Quakers, had established himself as a carpenter in the southwestern corner of Pennsylvania. There, in the Bridgeport Borough of Fayette near Brownsville, he was to own and operate a substantial sawing and planing mill.[2] Louis M. H. Wood, his third son, attended Waynesburg College in adjacent Greene County for two years and, in 1869, entered Cornell. At Cornell, he completed a second two years of study related to architecture. His education was through the civil engineering and mechanical arts programs of the college, in a gathering together of courses that immediately preceded the founding of Cornell's formal School of Architecture in June 1873. During his second year at Cornell, Louis Wood became the chief groundskeeper at the university and was placed in charge of the upkeep and repair of the five buildings that comprised the campus.[3] Louis' elder brother, Thomas, did not partake of the new training but rather learned the skills of sign painting, interior wall papering, wood graining, and

FIGURE 1. *John G. Haskell,*
ca. 1890s. (Kansas State
Historical Society, Topeka.)

glazing in the accepted generational tradition of father-to-son. Both men, his uncle Louis and his father Thomas, would be of significance in Hart Wood's early professional career.[4]

By autumn of 1871, after finishing at Cornell, Louis Wood began a westward migration that would be emulated by his brother Thomas. Like many, if not most, inexperienced architects coming out of the centuries-old farmer-carpenter social class, Louis sought opportunity—typically provided by either physical urban disaster or the exaggerated economics of boom times. The rebuilding of Chicago after the fire of 1871 drew Louis to that city. He stayed one year and moved again to Lawrence, Kansas. It is not known who he worked for as a draftsman in Chicago or why and how he sought and achieved employment in Lawrence.[5] World economic conditions, including those of the settled eastern United States, worsened dramatically in the early 1870s. Perhaps in anticipation of a depression that would ripple west, Louis Wood again followed some particular frontier opportunity. By 1873, he was working for John G. Haskell, an architect who by that year was the preeminent builder and designer for eastern Kansas and the Oklahoma Territory.[6]

In 1875, Louis Wood became Haskell's partner in the firm of Haskell and Wood (figs. 1–2). The partnership lasted about twelve years, until 1887. Haskell handled the business negotiations and supervised construction, while Wood took over the chief responsibilities of drafting and office routine. Among the significant commissions undertaken by the firm were the Kansas State Capitol (Topeka), 1866–1874, 1885, 1891–1893; the Chase County Courthouse (Cottonwood Falls, Kansas), 1871–1873; a number of buildings for Kansas University (Lawrence), Washburn University (Topeka), and the Haskell Institute (Lawrence); miscellaneous large-scale public buildings from Salina east to Kansas City and south to the Oklahoma border; and a group of federal agency schools for the Cherokee and Chilocco tribes in the Oklahoma Territory.[7] These years, 1872–1887, epitomized the experience of frontier opportunity sought by young architects such as Louis Wood. Such successes inspired others, and in about 1882 or 1883 Thomas Hart Benton Wood, Louis' brother, also went west to Kansas with his British wife Maggie and their young son Hart.[8]

Precisely why the second Wood family left the East remains unknown. Difficult work conditions in Philadelphia or perhaps letters of stability and continued good fortune from a brother two years junior may have stimulated the move. The Thomas H. B. Wood family likely stopped in Lawrence en route, staying with the Louis Wood family before going farther west to the frontier town of Hays, near the border of Kansas and Colorado.[9] At about age two, then, Hart Wood made the journey from a large coastal city in the Northeast to the sparsely settled high plains. By mid-May 1884, the Thomas H. B. Wood family had established themselves in Hays (fig. 3). Severe drought conditions had prevailed for the first years of the 1880s on the high plains, but by about 1884–1885 the climate again became more amenable to hopeful newcomers, and inexpensive rail fares enticed immigrants west. Thomas Wood went to Hays as the pastor for the Methodist Episcopal Church. The church had a small congregation of sixty-nine members in 1884–1885. By early 1886, he had become the pastor of the Lutheran Church in Hays, a church with a similar membership size during these years. In 1887, Thomas Wood advertised himself as a house-and-sign painter and paper hanger, with his own shop in town. He expanded his business into graining and glazing by 1889.[10] "Sign painting" during the late-nineteenth and early-twentieth centuries was a catchall term for a profession that included not only painting but all types of interior design. A sign painter often was versed in the crafts of graining, glazing, murals, and fresco.[11] His pattern of mal-

FIGURE 2. *Louis M. H. Wood, ca. 1890. (Kansas State Historical Society, Topeka.)*

FIGURE 3. *Main Street, Hays, Kansas, 1880. (Kansas Room, Hays Public Library.)*

leable employment reflected the harsh boom-and-bust cycles of 1880s western Kansas. Survival in an extremely uneven economy demanded that Thomas Wood use as many of his skills as possible.

The Thomas Wood family spent about six years in Hays. The town was the seat of government for Ellis County, a thirty-square-mile area that included five Russian-German settlements founded in 1876–1877 (Catherine, just south of Hays, and Herzog, Munjor, Pfeifer, and Schoenchen). These communities maintained a focus on religious life—both Catholic and Lutheran—and sought out German-speaking priests and pastors.[12] As for business, the years 1883–1886 were rainy ones on the high plains and thus were good years for the fragile land-based economy. However, by 1887 the economy had begun to falter, with the "great bust of 1888" only an opener to a period of very difficult years. Everything failed. Drought came, deepening in the 1890s. Hot, dry, windy summers stimulated articles in *Harper's Monthly* on the Great American Desert. Snow, more wind, and cold temperatures arrived with winter's vengeance.

Agriculture and ranching collapsed. People left the area. The total population in Kansas west of the 100th meridian was 81,279 in 1889; by 1895, only 49,850 people remained.[13] By the autumn of 1890, the Thomas H. B. Wood family joined the exodus, moving farther west to Denver.[14]

Two conditions appear to have influenced the Denver move, each reinforcing the negative circumstances present in western Kansas. The first condition affected many people who were looking for new opportunities: Denver was in the midst of a silver-based boom that had begun in 1888.[15] The second condition, however, was particular to the Wood family dynamics. Louis Wood had left Haskell and Wood in 1887 for Topeka and by 1889 had set up practice in Denver.[16] Once more, Thomas Wood followed his younger brother west. In December 1890, Hart Wood turned ten. He had gone west as a very young child and had, in all probability, spent some time in the household of his architect-uncle Louis as a toddler and during visits of 1884–1890. Of equal note, Hart had survived the harsh years in Hays while of an age to remember them. As a complement to the severity of life on the high plains, he had also experienced firsthand the fragile, presettlement ecosystem of the region: unbroken sod, waving high grasses, wildflowers in profusion, abundant and varied fauna. Western Kansas should have had an unforgettable impact, particularly with respect to nature, land forms, climate, and the balance of built environment with virgin landscape. Pristine qualities of color, line, and texture must have dominated rural Kansans' life as well.[17]

Paralleling the move from Philadelphia to Kansas, the move from Kansas to Denver presented another radical life change for the boy Hart Wood. Denver supported continuous construction between 1888 and 1894, with a dynamic Richardsonian Romanesque defining the downtown (fig. 4). During the winter of 1895–1896, the regional mining town of Leadville became the location of a five-acre ice palace that showcased the products of Colorado in a tradition derived from Russia (and continued in the 1880s and 1890s in Montreal, Quebec, Ottawa, and Saint Paul) (fig. 5).[18] The preteen and early teen years were traditionally ones of apprenticeship for the building trades. Hart Wood likely received some familial training from his uncle Louis and his father Thomas. Architectural office skills learned from Louis Wood during his formative years were doubtless significant, yet not more so than the painting, graining, and glazing crafts mastered through his father's tutelage at home. From 1889 through 1894, Louis Wood was one of thirty-one architects in Denver. Thomas Wood worked in the city during these same years as a "sign writer."[19] Throughout this period, the spirit of what architecture could become in a fresh western city enlivened Denver's community of hopeful—and highly successful—architects and draftsmen.

In early 1889, J. B. Dorman, a Denver journalist, founded *Western Architect and Building News* and called for the formation of a more tightly organized local art and architectural society. By the journal's second issue, the Denver Architectural Sketch Club had debuted. Denver's alliance·of artists focused on architects, but it also included a broad cross-spectrum of thinking citizens that ranged from the oft-disregarded engineers to the world of writers and politicians.[20] The Denver Architectural Sketch Club was one of the earlier such art clubs in the United States. The club began shortly after the civic art movement was given official notice in 1886 through the Architectural League of New York. A hallmark of the newly organizing American municipal art scene was its bringing together of architects, sculptors, and painters for public art. An annual exhibition through the joint efforts of club members was another noteworthy feature.[21]

In Denver, as was true across the nation, the most active members of the Architectural Sketch Club were not the established senior architects but rather the draftsmen who worked (sometimes as chief designers) for these

FIGURE 4. *Denver, ca. 1890s. (Colorado Historical Society, Denver.)*

FIGURE 5. *Charles E. Joy, Ice Palace, Leadville, Colorado, winter 1895–1896. (Colorado Historical Society, Denver.)*

architects. A key element of *Western Architect and Building News* became Denver's buildings, almost always presented through the draftsmen's drawings for them. A wide variety of articles on elements of public art also marked the journal, from discussions of landscape to building materials. The Denver Architectural Sketch Club, in combination with *Western Architect and Building News*, was the regional educational vehicle for young architects and architects-to-be during 1889–1891.[22] When the journal ceased publication in August 1891 due to funding problems, the architectural community took yet another organizational step. In December 1891, the Colorado Association of Architects met, voted for application as a chapter of the American Institute of Architects (AIA), and was granted such status in spring 1892. A sequential development following the city's Architectural Sketch Club and journal, the AIA chapter carried forward vibrant, nonacademic education among Denver's architects. The city's building ordinance and lien law were uppermost concerns in the 1890s.[23]

Hart Wood came of age in Denver during the 1890s. In addition to the intense atmosphere of the building boom and the educational values of the sketch club and its journal, Denver also offered an art school and the Artists' Club. The latter, run by Henry Read (1851–1935), intermingled with the Denver Architectural Sketch Club, as evidenced by its inclusion of architectural photographs and drawings at club exhibitions and meetings.[24] During 1894–1895, the Artists' Club showcased the work of Willis Adams Marean, an architect with whom Hart Wood would become employed. The Artists' Club also garnered subscriptions to multiple influential art journals through its members, journals including the *London Daily Graphic, Art Amateur* (New York), *Sun and Shade: An Artistic Periodical* (New York), *The London Studio*, the *Quarterly Illustrator* (New York), and the *Magazine of Art* (London and New York).[25]

Certainly, Hart Wood must have benefited from the many levels of

FIGURE 6. *Franklin School, Denver, ca. 1885–1890. (Colorado Historical Society, Denver.)*

artistic activity in Denver during these years. The supportive art community became especially significant after 1895, when the regional silver economy went bust. At this time, Hart's immediate family environment changed yet again. His uncle Louis Wood left Denver, returning to Topeka where he would practice for the duration of his career. His father Thomas Wood ceased listing himself as a sign writer in the Denver directories in 1894. From this year forward, Thomas Wood worked as a janitor in Denver—first at Central School and then at Franklin School.[26] In 1898, Hart Wood lived at Franklin School (fig. 6) with his father, working for the Denver architects Marean and Norton. Other Wood family members continued to reside at Franklin School into the early twentieth century.[27]

WOOD'S EARLY CAREER

2

By 1897 or 1898, Hart Wood had formally entered the architectural profession, inaugurating his career through Marean & Norton and Frank E. Edbrooke & Company. The Edbrooke firm was responsible for much of Denver's late-nineteenth-century appearance, with the Brown Palace Hotel of 1892 considered a masterpiece of art and engineering (fig. 7). Edbrooke & Company also had trained many of the region's architects, including Willis Adams Marean and Albert Julius Norton.[1] Frank E. Edbrooke (1840–1921) was one of three prominent architect sons of English builder Robert J. Edbrooke. The Edbrooke family had played an active role in the rebuilding of Chicago after the 1871 fire before moving to Denver in 1879.[2] Willis Adams Marean (1853–1939) came to Denver in 1880 from New York, where he had run a contracting business and worked as a draftsman. Between 1880 and 1895, Marean assumed a lead design position within Edbrooke & Company, with Edbrooke the superintendent for the firm's construction. Marean participated in Read's Artists' Club as one of its most active members. He was also known for his collection of Japanese and Chinese porcelains, bronzes, lacquers, and paintings and was "deeply versed" in "the arts of the Orient."[3]

Albert Julius Norton (1867–1944) had earned a BS in architecture

FIGURE 7. *Frank E. Edbrooke and Company, Brown Palace Hotel, Denver, 1890–1892. (Colorado Historical Society, Denver.)*

at Cornell—an early formal degree in the profession—and had worked
briefly for firms in New York and Boston before arriving in Denver in
1890. Norton, too, first worked for Edbrooke & Company. Willis Marean
and Albert Norton left Edbrooke's firm simultaneously in 1895, forming
the partnership Marean & Norton that year. Norton often traveled in
Europe and like Marean participated in Denver's fine art circles. Marean
& Norton involved themselves in Denver's public art in particular. Willis
Marean and Henry Read both contributed to Frederick Law Olmsted's
design of Denver's parks and parkways.[4] In early 1897, immediately
before Hart Wood's hiring as a draftsman for Marean & Norton, the
Denver Artists' Club requested the design of an "appropriate meeting
facility" from its architect members. Marean & Norton's drawings for the
Artists' Club building were among those of five Denver firms exhibited at
an open public meeting of late January 1897.[5]

The regional prominence of Edbrooke & Company and Marean
& Norton during the last twenty years of the nineteenth century was
strikingly similar to that of John G. Haskell's Kansas firm, 1865–1900.
Indeed, the three firms—Edbrooke's, Marean & Norton's, and
Haskell's—could be described as epitomizing adjacent spheres of
regional architectural influence, with the tenure of the earlier firm
overlapping that of the later firm farther west. Hart Wood began his
long architectural career with Marean & Norton.[6] By 1900, at about
age twenty, he was a draftsman for Edbrooke & Company, staying until
sometime in late 1901 or early 1902.[7]

In 1902, Hart Wood established himself anew in California.[8] His
reasons for relocating are unknown, but once in San Francisco his
artistic growth was inevitable. Wood went to work for English architect
Charles E. Hodges at Stanford University. Hodges had previously been
an employee of Shepley, Rutan & Coolidge, the Boston architects for

the university. In a January 1902 letter to Jane Stanford, wife of the
university's founder, Hodges mentioned hiring two extra draftsmen
to handle the enormous building activity then underway. During late
1901 and 1902, the mechanical engineering laboratory, the southeast
corner building, the museum extension, the gymnasium, Memorial
Church, and the library were all in active drafting or construction.[9] Hart
Wood's previous experience was appropriate to the campus project.
Shepley, Rutan & Coolidge had designed the sandstone buildings in a
style that was the forerunner of California's Mission Revival, combining
Richardsonian Romanesque detail with Franciscan Mission form and
plan. By coincidence, Denver's conservatism at the turn of the century
meshed with the innovative Stanford University design of 1886, which in
turn had become extremely conservative in its final building campaigns
of the early twentieth century. And for the second time, Wood found
himself exposed to landscape architecture through the picturesque
layout of Frederick Law Olmsted. Located near Menlo Park (Palo Alto),
south of San Francisco on the peninsula, Stanford University must have
made quite an impression on Wood. The campus design of low, powerful
buildings and groves of eucalyptus was among the more significant in the
West. For Hart Wood, it was a good beginning on the Pacific Coast.

By late 1902 or early 1903, with the building rush under control
at Stanford, Wood accepted a position in San Francisco with the just-
established firm of Meyer and O'Brien. The atmosphere was one of
young architects and fresh images. Meyer was 27, O'Brien 34, Wood
only 22. As at Stanford, Hart Wood's tenure with Meyer and O'Brien was
short—a year or less. Yet the experience was again significant. Frederick
H. Meyer was the son of a cabinetmaker, apprenticed to his father during
his youth. Meyer had a strong feeling for wood craftsmanship and detail.
Perhaps not coincidentally, Hart Wood's own talents would prove

similar. During 1902, Meyer and O'Brien designed the Rialto Building in San Francisco. Exposure to this project, possibly including some contribution to the building's design, was a fine second California step for Wood. The earthquake and fire of 1906 destroyed the Rialto. In 1910, Bliss and Faville was responsible for the reconstruction of the building to the original Meyer and O'Brien design. By this year, Hart Wood was an employee of Bliss and Faville, and it is possible that he worked on the commission twice. If he played a design role in 1902, Wood may well have been the reason that Bliss and Faville received the commission in 1910.[10]

By 1904, Hart Wood had joined the firm of Bliss and Faville, perhaps the most important step in his career during the pre-Hawaii years.[11] The Bliss family name poses several unanswered questions. The most critical of these questions is whether Walter D. Bliss (of Bliss and Faville) was related to Mary Elizabeth Bliss Haskell, the wife of John G. Haskell (of Haskell and Wood in Lawrence, Kansas). If so, it is possible that Hart Wood landed the job with Bliss and Faville via his uncle Louis Wood.[12] Mary Elizabeth's brother John A. moved from Wilbraham, Massachusetts, to Lawrence, Kansas, in 1868 and then to California in 1884. John A. Bliss settled in Oakland in 1888. Walter D. Bliss and several of his siblings also lived in Oakland after the turn of the century. In 1904, John A. Bliss, by then a member of the California Dairy Bureau and an assemblyman representing the 15th District, returned to Lawrence to visit his sister Mary Elizabeth. If Mary Elizabeth Bliss is the same person as Mary Elizabeth Bliss Haskell, then it is probable that John A. Bliss knew the Louis and Thomas Wood families during the early 1880s when he too had lived in Lawrence. John A. Bliss may have asked about the Woods families and discovered that Hart Wood had grown up to be an architect—and was a young practicing professional in San Francisco. In any case, Bliss and Faville (Walter D. Bliss) hired Hart Wood in 1904, the identical year of the John A. Bliss family trip back to Lawrence.[13]

Hart Wood's tenure with Bliss and Faville included exposure to and participation in several major commissions in San Francisco. The St. Francis Hotel, under construction in 1904, was one of the first Bliss and Faville projects after Wood's arrival at the firm. Following the San Francisco earthquake of 1906, Bliss and Faville moved their offices into the hotel to supervise its rebuilding and additions. Work at the St. Francis continued for a number of years, with *Architect and Engineer of California* citing Bliss and Faville commissions for wings and a planned tower at the hotel, 1907–1912. The two original wings were rebuilt by late 1907, with the St. Francis' masterful interior work completed by 1909.

Certainly the size of the St. Francis project must have served as a testing ground for Wood. Yet, more critically, the elaborate interior of the hotel must have opened up new vistas for the architect—vistas of color, materials, and texture. In particular, the use of heavy timbered ceilings, contrasting woods (mahogany, walnuts, and oaks) stained and stenciled with color (copper, reds, and blues), as well as paneling heavily sandblasted or grained to catch the light, were all design features that would appear in Hart Wood's later work. One other keynote of the St. Francis commission was the roof garden above the third wing of the hotel (1910). As this addition was likely one in which Wood did have a major active part, it may mark his earliest effort at architectonic landscape design.[14] Work on the St. Francis during 1907–1912 provides the first graphic reference to Hart Wood's family training in the craft of architectural interiors, while also illustrating his sensitivity to landscape and to the more abstract issues of light and color in the built environment (fig. 8).

During these first years with Bliss and Faville, several changes occurred in Wood's personal life. By 1904 Wood was living in the East

FIGURE 8. *Bliss and Faville/ Hart Wood, St. Francis Hotel, San Francisco, 1907–1912.* Architect and Engineer of California, *January 1914.*

Bay—first in Berkeley, then in Oakland, and finally in Piedmont. The Berkeley-Oakland hills evoked a more picturesque, outdoor California lifestyle than did downtown San Francisco. In the easternmost sections of Berkeley and Oakland, the atmosphere was almost rural. Steep hillsides offered stunning, unblemished views of the bay. Foliage was thick (or could be made so), and other houses were few. The East Bay was also home to a distinct group of architects. In Berkeley, Bernard Maybeck, with his individualistic designs for rustic residences, stood out. Due to a building depression in Honolulu, Charles William Dickey also opened an office in Oakland in 1903: Dickey and Reed.[15] Without doubt, the small coterie of East Bay architects knew each other, developing stronger ties as the century began to unfold.

On November 21, 1906, Hart Wood married Jessie Spangler in Berkeley, honeymooning in Southern California. On the occasion of his marriage, local press described him as "an architect of ability . . . [with] . . . a most promising future."[16] Hart's sister Gertrude, a musician, came from Denver to attend the wedding.[17] The marriage sustained Wood's ties to the Midwest. His wife's family was originally from Illinois, Missouri, and Kansas, where his father-in-law Emmons R. Spangler had run a hardware business.[18]

The years 1906–1908 were an important developmental period for Hart Wood. In 1906, Bliss and Faville undertook the commission for the Bank of California in San Francisco. *Architectural Record* carried a presentation drawing of the bank in June, discussing the similarity of its design to McKim, Mead and White's Knickerbocker Trust Company building erected in New York in 1904. Hart subsequently listed this project as the earliest commission among a group of Bliss and Faville designs he claimed as chiefly his own work. The drawing may be from Wood's hand, but if so it exhibits a style far different from that evident in the architect's signed work of just several years later. Regardless, the architect likely did have a major role in the bank's design. A stout, Classical form, the Bank of California is indeed a well-done mimic of the Knickerbocker Trust. Although the Knickerbocker Trust was originally designed to carry a skyscraper of thirteen stories, its heavy, ornate character was intrinsic to the high style of McKim, Mead and White. In the San Francisco bank, Bliss and Faville simplified the design detail and paid careful attention to the articulation of all corners and outer edges. The architects pulled in and stepped back elements of the design to create a tighter whole, one anchored and unified in a way that subtly alluded to a different artistic direction.[19]

The Bank of California offers a first look at Hart Wood's personal evolution away from the pristine Beaux Arts (fig. 9). By the close of 1908, Hart Wood had likely become Bliss and Faville's chief designer. In biographical statements of the following years, the architect referred to his multiyear position with the San Francisco firm as that of head draftsman. The difficulty remains in projecting when Hart Wood's status changed from that of one draftsman within a group to that of the supervising draftsman for the firm. The shift probably occurred during work on the Bank of California project. By this time, signed "Hart Wood" presentation drawings existed that officially represented Bliss and Faville.[20] The firm's drawing style for commissions prior to 1908 is markedly different than after that date.

Between 1908 and 1914, Bliss and Faville achieved a plateau of excellence. Their commissions included the Columbia (later Geary) Theater (1908–1909), the Savings Union Bank and Trust Company (later Security Pacific Bank) (1909), continued work on the St. Francis Hotel (1910–1912), the Masonic Temple (1910–1912), the Children's Hospital (1910), and contributions to the Panama Pacific International Exposition (1913–1914). During these years, Bliss and Faville enjoyed increasing recognition for its work, with critiques in *American Architect* and *Architectural Record*.[21] In addition to wide press, Bliss and Faville began to receive invitations to enter national competitions for large, prestigious commissions. Among these were the Denver Federal Building competition of 1909, the Washington, D.C., Department of Justice Building competition of 1910, and the United States Treasury Department Post Office competition for Portland, Oregon, of 1913.[22] All of the Bliss and Faville designs claimed by Hart Wood between 1908

FIGURE 9. *Bliss and Faville/Hart Wood,*
Bank of California, San Francisco, 1906.
Architectural Record, *June 1906.*

and 1914 evoked a continued McKim, Mead and White tradition of
Beaux Arts classicism.[23] In the Columbia Theater and the Savings Union
Bank, temple facades with colossal colonnades, pediments, and domes
echoed the Greek and Roman classicism of the Bank of California.
In the Children's Hospital and the Masonic Temple, form and detail
recalled the Renaissance palazzo, drawing upon another strain of Beaux
Arts classicism and pointing back to the St. Francis Hotel. However,
whereas the Bank of California and the St. Francis Hotel had offered
emphatic tributes to the New York firm with which both Walter D. Bliss
and William B. Faville had trained, the designs of this period—in which
Wood was more involved—stood apart. Conveyed in an innovative
drawing presentation style, these buildings coupled a Beaux Arts
vocabulary with an intense color palette, concentrations of sculptural
detail, and an urban architectonic landscape concern.

With the commission for the Columbia Theater, Hart Wood, then
twenty-eight, demonstrated his artistic independence. Overwhelmingly,
the building was a statement of color—and it remains so today.
Breaking with the linear style used in the drawings for the Bank of
California, Wood created a watercolor presentation drawing for the
Columbia Theater. August G. Headman, president of the San Francisco
Architectural Club, noted the unusual use of color for the drawing in
his review of the club's 1909 exhibition.[24] Illustrated in the *Yearbook* for
the show, the watercolor was uncut, with Hart Wood's signature in the
lower left corner. (*Architect and Engineer of California* featured the same
watercolor in January 1909 but cropped the drawing. The professional
journal removed Wood's signature and added a line crediting Bliss and
Faville.)[25] Color did more than highlight the presentation drawing. Deep
blues, purples, greens, browns, and oranges dominated the main facade
and interior of the structure itself. Faced with cream-colored pressed

brick, the Geary Street facade erupted in riotous color through the polychrome terra-cotta of its twisted columns, panels, architraves, and urns. Not only was the color intense, but Bliss and Faville also employed color in such a way as to throw columns, capitals, and cornices into high relief. The iconography of the building further broke with the restrained classicism of McKim, Mead and White. The columns overflowed with a cornucopia of ripe grapes, open pods of peas, pumpkins, and other greenery. On the interior, ornate plasterwork with Utah Caen stone and Tennessee marble complemented the color and texture of the facade. Interestingly, contemporary discussions of the commission described it as "distinctly classic and dignified," making only general allusions to the role of color and no references to iconography (figs. 10 and 11).[26]

During 1909–1912, the commissions of Bliss and Faville continued to pull away from the influences of McKim, Mead and White. The San Francisco Savings Union Bank and Trust Company of June 1909 maintained an allegiance to Beaux Arts tradition but simultaneously further explored directions initiated with the Bank of California. The Savings Union Bank functioned with its civic neighbors—the Phelan Building of 1908 by William Curlett and the Union Trust Company of 1910 by Clinton Day (later the Wells Fargo Bank)—as a City Beautiful gateway to Grant Avenue. The design of the bank also recalled several McKim, Mead and White variants on the Roman Pantheon, including Columbia University Library (1893), New York University Library (1896), the Bank of Montreal (1904), Madison Square Presbyterian Church in New York (1906), and the Girard Trust Company in Philadelphia (1908). Yet the imposing mass of the structure was fundamentally different from that of the mainstream Beaux Arts. The Savings Union Bank was a sculpturally tight design, appearing almost as if carved from a single block of stone. What had been tentative in the Bank

FIGURE 10. *Columbia (later Geary) Theater, San Francisco. (David Franzen, 1984.)*

of California was crystallized in the Savings Union Bank. Each section of the design stepped back from its adjacent section in an upward direction toward the dome itself. Corner modulation especially bespoke a unit simplicity. Columns did not extend to the corners, making the building's edges clear, sharp, and rectilinear. In the San Francisco Savings Union Bank, Hart Wood opened his lifelong dialogue with the ground-hugging or ground-anchored form (fig. 12).[27]

In February and September 1910, Bliss and Faville began work

FIGURE 11. Opposite. *Bliss and Faville/Hart Wood, Columbia (later Geary) Theater, San Francisco, 1908–1909. (David Franzen, 1984.)*

FIGURE 12. Above. *Bliss and Faville/Hart Wood, Savings Union Bank (later Security Pacific Bank), San Francisco, 1909. (David Franzen, 1984.)*

FIGURE 13. *Bliss and Faville/ Hart Wood, Masonic Temple, San Francisco, 1910–1912. Photograph of a watercolor signed "Hart Wood." (Collection of Thomas Plant Contractors, San Francisco.)*

on the Children's Hospital and Masonic Temple in San Francisco. The hospital harkened back to a more Italianate classicism, again familiar to Wood through the traditions of McKim, Mead and White. A brick structure with a tile roof, the Children's Hospital was a much quieter design than either the Columbia Theater or the Savings Union Bank. Emphasis was on the textured effect of the face-brick, terra-cotta details, and "weather-beaten" roof tile. The U-shaped plan of the structure offered a street facade courtyard with stairs cascading from either side of the entry arch. The courtyard, like the roof garden for the St. Francis Hotel addition of 1910, reflected Wood's concern for the urban outdoor space. The design for the hospital richly concentrated exterior sculpture around doors and windows.[28]

By autumn 1910, Hart Wood was also actively working on drawings for the Masonic Temple, a commission that exceeded $750,000 in value. Like the presentation drawing for the Columbia Theater, the watercolor rendering of the temple was beautifully done and signed by Hart Wood. Several of the ink-on-linen drawings, with pencil detailing, were also initialed "HW."[29] The Masonic Temple combined the brilliant color of the Columbia Theater and the sculptural, ground-anchored form of the Savings Union Bank with the textured surfaces and clustered exterior detailing of the Children's Hospital in a tour de force that came closest to a full aesthetic break with the Beaux Arts work of McKim, Mead and White (figs.13–16). The structure took three years to complete. In December 1913, three hundred San Francisco architects, engineers, and draftsmen were invited for a formal inspection of the building. *Architect and Engineer of California* reported that Bliss and Faville received many compliments for their stunning work.[30]

The interior and exterior of the Masonic Temple was a study in contrasts. Color was largely confined to the interior—but what an

FIGURE 14. *Bliss and Faville/ Hart Wood, Masonic Temple, San Francisco, 1910–1912. Ink on linen drawing of 13 September 1911. (Collection of Thomas Plant Contractors, San Francisco.)*

FIGURE 15. *Bliss and Faville/Hart Wood,*
Masonic Temple, San Francisco, 1910–
1912. Lodge room ceiling detail. (David
Franzen, 1984.)

interior it was! The second lodge room extensively employed carved wood paneling, with multiple inset color details. Opaquely painted, the insets gave the compositions a flat, almost Japanese quality. Deep orange, a blue-green, mustard yellow, red, white, tan, and a lighter green dazzled the eye. Figures set in the woodwork had a washed quality, similar to watercolor. The pilasters and capitals at all corners used color, and each composition was slightly different from the others. The coffered ceiling featured multiple levels of paneled recession and depended heavily on color and texture for its effects. A green stain finished the major coffered panels, while light and dark natural woods were inset as details. The two-story height of the space further enhanced its magnificence. The main lodge room also offered an expansive space, but instead of presenting color the room offered texture. Dark wood paneled the walls, accented with recessed niches. For the ceiling, the architect relied on a scheme of decorated beams. Plaster beams approximately three feet wide marched across the ceiling, with narrower beams placed between them. A dark wood painted graining finished the beams, with the wide beams decorated in grape and foliage motifs. Other details within the interior emphasized a richness of color, texture, materials, and concentrated ornament.[31] In counterpoint, the exterior of the Masonic Temple gave the impression, like the Savings Union Bank, of a single carved unit—here almost fortresslike. Described by the architectural press as "Florentine," the exterior facades featured recessed window arches, a first-story false arcade, rectangular screenwork between stories, triple-arched openings set apart by variants of twisted columns, a heavy cornice with quatrefoil motif, and a standing, canopied figure at the building's corner, projecting outward. Sculpted figures intensely covered the main entrance to the Masonic Temple, creating a formal portal reminiscent of medieval cathedrals.

FIGURE 16. *Masonic Temple, San Francisco, 1910–1912. Bas-relief detail. (David Franzen, 1984.)*

Between 1910 and 1912, Hart Wood not only achieved a plateau of excellence with Bliss and Faville, but he also became more deeply involved in the architectural community of the East Bay. In November 1910, Wood founded the Oakland Architectural Club, serving as its president from 1910 through 1912. Other officers included E. B. Mead and W. J. Wilkinson, with directors John Galen Howard, Louis C. Mullgardt, Oswald Spier, and C. E. Richardson. By August 1911, a second Oakland organization had also formed—the Oakland Architects' Society—shortly to be renamed the Oakland Architectural Association. That group's first president was Louis S. Stone. Charles W. Dickey served as its vice president. Members of the Oakland Architectural Association included John Bakewell, J. J. Donovan, C. W. McCall, H. C. Smith, and the Newsom brothers. Both organizations existed only briefly: the Oakland Architectural Club until November 1912 and the Oakland Architectural Association until August 1913.[32] The two-year life of each, however, signaled an independent architectural current in the East Bay.[33]

Most of the Oakland club members lived in Berkeley, Piedmont, and Oakland, but only a few actually practiced in their home communities. San Francisco was the professional base for nearly all. Yet a purposeful idealism and artistic unity characterized the East Bay group, distinct from their affiliation and employment with the large, traditional architectural firms in San Francisco. Both the Oakland Architectural Club and Oakland Architectural Association had hoped to sponsor activities similar to the art and architectural clubs in San Francisco that had mentored them. But it was not until the Oakland architects banded together a second time, in a single organized event of 1916, that a formal exhibition and catalogue appeared. The exhibition pulled all the Oakland and Berkeley area architects together. In the 1916 show, Hart Wood's work (then as Wood and Simpson) figured heavily. Charles

W. Dickey chaired the committee that made the selections for the exhibition.[34]

In February 1911, Hart Wood received his certificate to practice architecture in California, an official indicator that his draftsman days were nearing a close.[35] A second, unofficial sign came in 1912, when Hart designed his own house high in the Piedmont hills. Erected on a steep incline, facing Dracena Park to the north and the Pacific Ocean to the west, the house was one of only a few in the immediate vicinity. Built into the hillside, partially on a massive concrete block foundation, the house offered uninterrupted views of the bay and its surrounding hills. The siting of the residence, with its rear and side garden spaces, emphatically conveyed the architect's feelings for nature and landscape. The design of the Hart Wood house, however, was the more striking revelation. Rustic, shingled, and irregular in plan and elevation, with an open upper-story porch supported by redwood columns, the house paid homage to Bernard Maybeck, Ernest Coxhead, and Willis Polk (fig. 17). The wooden columns, each still sheathed in bark, gave a simple majesty to the informal design. Wood's sons used the porch for sleeping in good weather. A hinged double door set low in the paneling of the dining room allowed the children to slide a bed out onto the porch, and when open it improved ventilation throughout the house.

Although a modest house, the Hart Wood residence in Piedmont featured numerous crafted details. The living room ceiling reflected the slope of the gable roof and was dramatically steep. Its dark beams contrasted vividly against a plaster background, while the suspended crossbeam provided a secondary accent. The focal point in the room was a brick fireplace with a heavy wooden mantel. A small built-in bookcase bracketed the fireplace on one side, and a hidden bottle-glass window stepped up *inside* the fireplace on the other. In the dining room, the light

FIGURE 17. *Hart Wood, Hart Wood residence, Piedmont, California, 1912. (David Franzen, 1984.)*

from the square bay window to the west offset simple, dark paneling. Additional light filtered through the glass doors between the living and dining rooms to the east, further showcasing the woodwork.[36] Hart Wood's house, like the Oakland Architectural Club, symbolized not only the geographic separation between the East Bay and San Francisco but, more profoundly, the intellectual chasm between the worlds they represented.

Wood lived with the spirited avant-garde regionalism of the Maybeck circle, while he designed for Bliss and Faville in the Beaux Arts shadow of McKim, Mead and White. And to both approaches, he took his own talents.

During the exceptionally full months of 1911 and 1912—while Wood concentrated on the Masonic Temple for Bliss and Faville, chaired the Oakland Architectural Club, took his licensing exam, and designed his own East Bay house—another large-scale project was under way: the Panama-Pacific International Exposition. The world's fair was to be held in San Francisco during 1915, in honor of the completion of the Panama Canal. Fund-raising began in 1911. Simultaneously, the president of the exposition requested that the San Francisco chapter of the American Institute of Architects (AIA) select five of its members to become the fair's permanent architectural commission. Disagreements within this group of architects stimulated the selection of a new commission in 1912. The final architectural commission for the Panama-Pacific International Exposition included three New York architects, five San Francisco architects, and one architect from Los Angeles: Carrere and Hastings, McKim, Mead and White, and Henry Bacon (New York); Bliss and Faville, Bakewell and Brown, George W. Kelham, Louis Christian Mullgardt, and Ward and Blohm (San Francisco); and Robert David Farquhar (Los Angeles). Bernard Maybeck informally joined the commission at a later date.[37]

Bliss and Faville designed the Great Wall of the exposition, a wall sixty-five feet high connecting eight of the twelve palaces. The architectural press described the entire composition as "one vast building." The Bliss and Faville palaces designed for the Panama-Pacific International Exposition were those of Varied Industries, Manufacturers, Liberal Arts, Education, Food Products, Agriculture, Transportation, and Mines. As William B. Faville himself noted, the firm's work included

"the interiors, outer walls, domes and the walls forming the passageways
connecting the various courts." Bliss and Faville designed the entrances in
the Great Wall as points of accent, richly complex in detail. San Francisco
architect Bernard J. S. Cahill aptly commented on the wall, following
a showing of the drawings at the 1913 exhibition of the San Francisco
Architectural Club. Cahill described the Great Wall as "a simple band of
restful wall surface punctured at various quite unmonotonous intervals
with grilles, windows, niches and doors. Sometimes it gathers itself
up into a fortress-like tower gate, or quiets down to a simple Arch of
Triumph, or hollows itself into a great half dome, or breaks out into
gorgeous screens of richly wrought panelings, canopies and open
arcades." In addition to the Great Wall, Bliss and Faville also designed
the enclosing fence, a twenty-foot-high, double iceplant hedge, eight
feet deep and 1,150 feet long. For the hedge, the architects worked with
landscape genius John McLaren, the designer of Golden Gate Park. In
1911, the fair's organizers had appointed McLaren chief of the fair's
Department of Landscape Gardening.[38]

Designed by some of America's best Beaux Arts architects, the
Panama-Pacific International Exposition, dubbed "the Golden City,"
was a masterful urban environment that crowned the City Beautiful
Movement. Hart Wood, as chief draftsman for Bliss and Faville, cited
the exposition as among those projects on which he worked heavily.[39]
The Bliss and Faville contributions to the fair substantiate this claim.
The emphatic concentration of rich sculptural detail at the portals of the
Great Wall, punched forward by the stark simplicity of the wall itself,
was characteristic of much of Wood's work and could be seen developing
in his previous designs for the firm. William L. Woollett, in a review
of the exposition in 1915 for *Architectural Record*, described the wall's
detailing as "static" but noted that the sculptural portals were "poems

of ornament. "[40] Through the treatment of massing, as well as the duets of plane and ornament, Bliss and Faville's work at the Panama-Pacific International Exposition moved steadfastly away from the Beaux Arts of McKim, Mead and White. Much of the credit for this may be attributed to Hart Wood's infatuation with ornamentation and detail and to his facile capacity in creating architectural vignettes. Distinct from his collaboration within the firm, Hart Wood made his own artistic statement at the fair most clearly through color and landscape.

From as early as 1914, the architectural journals began to comment on the superb color of the exposition. And although Hart Wood did not devise the fair's palette, he appears to have played a pronounced role through his designs for Bliss and Faville. The portal of the Palace of Varied Industries derived from the Salamanca Cathedral, yet as observing critics were quick to note, there was no color in the original, and for the exposition portal there were blues, reds, and browns. Woollett elaborated on his discussion of the Great Wall portals, describing them as "gems of . . . harmonious color." By late 1915, two additional articles treating the issue of color at the Panama-Pacific International Exposition had appeared in *Architectural Record*. By mid-1916, *American Architect* further commented on the exposition's color, emphasizing that it was time to introduce color to colorless American architecture.[41]

Color was also the dominant element of the landscaping for the exposition. John McLaren employed a succession of California wildflowers, high in color, to complement his landscaping of the fair grounds: The Panama-Pacific International Exposition opened in a blaze of yellows. And it was also through landscape design that Hart Wood made his most memorable contribution to the fair: an architectonic landscape brilliant in hue, the twenty-foot high, enclosing iceplant hedge. The multiarched Beaux Arts living wall of dense green foliage, set heavily with pink blossoms, was a feat of architectural design, engineering, and landscape. Both Hart Wood and John McLaren claimed it as their work, and they probably designed it together. McLaren gathered all the specimens for the landscaping of the grounds during 1912 and 1913, nurturing them in a complex of greenhouses in the Tennessee Hollow of the Presidio Reservation. For the iceplant hedge, men took cuttings from all over the Bay Area and planted them in 8,700 two-by-six-foot boxes, two feet deep, covered with wire mesh. After the cuttings had rooted, creating oversized green bricks, men placed the boxes on edge. They nailed the living bricks to the twenty-foot-high, eight-foot-deep, double-arched wall frame. Portals, arches, and simple detailing articulated the hedge. Elaborate Beaux Arts street lamps illuminated the main gateway. The hedge at the Panama-Pacific International Exposition was like nothing undertaken before it, and it was the single engineering achievement that the Hawaii chapter of the AIA entered onto their forms for Wood's nomination as a fellow in 1947. The iceplant hedge not only included the main entrance to the Panama-Pacific International Exposition, but the landscape feature defined the entire south front of the public space that contained the fair's pavilions. Pipes along the top of the hedge watered the green wall automatically (figs. 18 and 19).[42]

In September 1914, Hart Wood left Bliss and Faville, joining the staff of Lewis P. Hobart.[43] Several possibilities for the change suggest themselves. *Architect and Engineer of California* noted in October that the European war was affecting the American profession. The best-quality drafting instruments, vellum, and tracing paper, all imported, were no longer available. Even worse, a war-engendered building depression was setting in. By 1914, despite the nascent gala festivities of the Panama-Pacific International Exposition and the election of William B. Faville as a fellow in the AIA, hard times stood at the doorstep of Bliss and Faville.

FIGURE 18. *Hart Wood and John McLaren, iceplant hedge, Panama-Pacific International Exposition, San Francisco, 1915. Photograph of construction published in* American Architect, *6 January 1915.*

FIGURE 19. *Hart Wood and John McLaren, iceplant hedge, Panama-Pacific International Exposition, San Francisco, 1915. Photograph published in the* Architect, *July 1915.*

Between 1914 and 1916, the number of draftsmen going out on their
own, of partnerships dissolving, and of partnerships reforming was high.
The market was extremely unstable. *Architect and Engineer of California*
announced in October 1914 that a well-known San Francisco firm, one
whose business had exceeded $1 million of work per year during recent
years, was cutting all salaries from chief draftsman down by 30 percent.
It is quite likely that the referenced firm was Bliss and Faville and that
the referenced chief draftsman was Hart Wood.[44] The salary cut, coupled
with his hidden role of eminence during the immediately preceding
years, may have been too much to accept. Architect Wood, even with the
risks of uncertain times on the horizon, sought another position.

Lewis P. Hobart was only seven years older than Wood himself.
Educated at the University of California–Berkeley in 1893–1894, he
had also studied abroad at the American Academy in Rome in 1894
and 1895 and at the Beaux-Arts Institute of Design during 1900–1902.
Apprenticing in New York before coming to San Francisco in 1906,
Hobart was making a name for himself by 1914. And in that unlikely year,
he had work on the boards. In August, *Architect and Engineer of California*
noted that Hobart was just completing plans for the New Zealand
Building at the Panama-Pacific International Exposition. The $500,000
office for the Firemen's Fund Insurance Company in San Francisco
had been under way since March. Hobart also credited himself with a
number of elegant Beaux Arts mansions for the wealthy of Burlingame,
Hillsborough, and San Mateo. By 1915, the regional architectural press
described him as "uncommonly successful," with a "clientele that enables
him to do large and important work."[45] The leap from Bliss and Faville to
Lewis P. Hobart was not one of outstanding change. Hart Wood traded
one Beaux Arts, protocorporate firm for another—albeit for one having a
perhaps slightly fresher outlook and more immediate opportunity.

Wood's role with Hobart is not precisely understood. He may have been chief draftsman, or he may have been merely a staff member. Hart did not stay with Hobart long—at best no more than nine months—but within this brief period, the Hobart firm undertook the University of California Hospital in San Francisco ($600,000) and the U.S. Post Office in Portland ($1 million). These would have been significant commissions in good times, outstanding commissions in bad times. Wood likely participated to some degree on both these designs. Undertaken in September and October 1914, their timing almost assures Wood's role. In the case of the Portland Post Office, another curious fact emerges. Bliss and Faville had been awarded that commission in late 1913, but due to problems with the competition, it was reopened. A year later, Lewis P. Hobart received the commission. At the time of both awards, Hart Wood had been with the winning firm. It is possible he could have begun working on the design of the Portland Post Office while with Bliss and Faville in 1913 and continued working on it under Hobart during 1914–1915. Curiously, too, a watercolor of the post office was presented opposite two of Wood and Simpson's watercolors in the 1916 Alameda County Society of Architects *Yearbook*. The Portland Post Office watercolor may have been Wood's. (In 1916 the post office was still under construction.) The watercolor of the University of California Hospital, also published in the 1916 *Yearbook*, may have been Wood's as well.[46]

WOOD AND SIMPSON

WOOD OPENS HIS OWN FIRM

3

In July 1915, *Architect and Engineer of California* announced that Hart Wood and Horace G. Simpson had formed a partnership: Wood and Simpson.[1] Wood's reasons for leaving Hobart are shadowy. The business climate was steadily deteriorating, and the Portland Post Office commission was mired in federal bureaucracy. Hobart's bright outlook of autumn 1914 may have disappeared, along with the ability to keep all of his staff. Horace G. Simpson was a good partner for Wood. In the same month that Hart had announced his leave-taking of Bliss and Faville, Llewellyn B. Dutton, another established San Francisco architect, had announced his intention to retire from practice. His chief designer was Simpson, who by the close of 1914 was without a job.

Simpson, like Wood, was thirty-four and lived in the East Bay (Berkeley). He too was well versed in a Beaux Arts background. Simpson had handled major commissions while with Dutton, commissions parallel to those of Wood's with Bliss and Faville. By 1914, Simpson's design work had pulled away from the pure Beaux Arts, moving in an artistic direction that was quite distinctive, albeit neither as powerful nor as recognized as that of Wood's.[2] By the beginning of 1915, he had taken his licensing exam and had been awarded his certificate to practice architecture in California. By June, Simpson had applied for and was awarded membership in the San Francisco Chapter of the AIA.[3] The timing might have been excellent for both Hart Wood and Horace G. Simpson, except for the climate of World War I. Wartime scarcity engulfed the life of their firm during 1915–1917.

Times were lean, and during the first eight months of business the hopeful firm had no real work. Wood and Simpson did not receive any major commissions until 1916. These projects—the Santa Fe Building and the Randolph Apartments in San Francisco—were evocative of the tentative upsurge in the building market that year. They also reflected Wood's and Simpson's previous individual reputations as talented head draftsmen. Wood and Simpson undertook the commission for the Santa Fe Building, a twelve-story office on Market Street, in June. A steel-frame structure with red brick walls and white terra-cotta trim, the Santa Fe Building was a Beaux Arts design. On the interior, the first two floors featured white marble and bronze detailing, witnessing once again Wood's feeling for texture and contrasting materials. Engaged pilasters marched around the ground floor office in pairs, framing flat niches painted with scenes of the California missions. The allusion to regional architecture foreshadowed aspects of Hart Wood's later career in Hawaii (fig. 20).[4]

Wood and Simpson designed the Randolph Apartments (fig. 21) in a simplified Beaux Arts aesthetic. The firm undertook the commission in March 1916, several months prior to the Santa Fe Building. Sheathed in red brick with white trim, the apartments were almost Colonial Revival in tone. The urban residential commission opened Wood and Simpson's dialogue with planned housing, a thrust that would become preeminent for the firm. Five stories high, the Randolph Apartments included sixty units, divided into two- and three-room suites. Described as a "refreshing design"—one making the apartment seem more like a home—the

FIGURE 20. Opposite. *Wood and Simpson, Santa Fe Building, San Francisco, 1916– 1917. (David Franzen, 1984.)*

FIGURE 21. *Wood and Simpson, Randolph Apartments, San Francisco, 1916. (David Franzen, 1984.)*

building occupied less than half its lot. The rear units of the Randolph
Apartments, as well as the front ones, were adequately lit. Every kitchen
had direct outside light and ventilation. Courts, double the legal require-
ment in size, ventilated all bathrooms. Dressing rooms were also ventilated, although this was not mandatory. In the rear, a landscaped garden
with brick walks was a notable feature. Wood and Simpson kept the costs
low through their use of a compact plan.[5]

Wood and Simpson had opened their practice with a series of
articles (by Simpson) and of watercolors, drawings, and sketches (by
both Wood and Simpson) published in *Architect and Engineer of California* between October 1915 and March 1916. Each one's presentations
addressed issues of planned suburban and industrial housing. For both
architects, multiple-unit housing was a recent concern, although Hart
Wood may have worked on the initial designs for the Women's Republic
Community at Atascadero, California, while still with Bliss and Faville.
Commissioned in early 1913, the colony was to include administration, civic and industrial buildings, schools, a university, a plaza, and
an extensive park system. Atascadero, located 120 miles north of Santa
Barbara, spread across 23,000 acres inland from Morro Bay. The town
was strongly progressive and until 1915 was a utopian outpost of the
American Woman's Republic—first developed as a colony for single
women and their dependent children. Edward Gardner Lewis had moved
his art pottery from University City (in St. Louis, near the grounds of the
1904 world's fair) to Atascadero. The California town was Lewis' final
community project. The planning board set up for Atascadero included
Walter D. Bliss, as well as Arts and Crafts horticulturist Edward J. Wick-
son of Berkeley. The board forbade billboards and barn advertisements.
As envisioned, Atascadero was to be a model exhibit, seen by visitors
traveling by train between the Panama-Pacific International Exposition

in San Francisco (1915) and the Panama-California Exposition in San Diego (1915–1916). Lewis had hoped to have Atascadero ablaze in electric lights as the Southern Pacific passed nightly.[6] For a variety of reasons, construction of the town fell behind schedule. Although Wood's role in this project, if any, remains unknown, his exposure to such a project in 1913, coupled with the urban planning experience offered by his work on the Panama-Pacific International Exposition, may have focused some of his thoughts on the pressing housing questions of the era.[7]

Simpson began writing articles for *Architect and Engineer of California* in October 1915. His first published essay, "An English Cottage at the [Panama-Pacific International] Exposition," discussed his Holt Manufacturing Pavilion. He had designed the building the year before while working for Llewellyn B. Dutton. Simpson made a plea for the "English Cottage" (Tudor Revival), noting that the style was "pre-eminently fitted to the purposes of country and suburban life." Accompanying the architect's argument were photographs of the beautifully detailed Holt Pavilion, along with his signed drawings for the commission. The essay also served as a subtle advertisement for the new firm of Wood and Simpson. The next article appeared in December 1915, entitled "Residence Sub-Division—Its Relation to Urban Development and to Architecture." Illustrated with recent examples of English suburban "garden-city" houses, the second Simpson essay in *Architect and Engineer of California* featured a frontispiece watercolor for "A House in Piedmont." The watercolor was executed in the presentation style established by Hart Wood (fig. 22).[8]

Apparently never built, the mansion planned for Piedmont was Tudor Revival in its design. Evocative of a new direction, the design was a logical extension of the sculptural, ground-anchored forms designed by Bliss and Faville for the Savings Union Bank and the Masonic Temple. For the Piedmont house, however, the emphasis was horizontal, the form

FIGURE 22. *Wood and Simpson, "A House in Piedmont," watercolor published in* Architect and Engineer of California, *December 1915.*

carved out of the ground itself. The feeling was entirely English. The simplicity of massing, form, and detail present in the Piedmont house was strongly reminiscent of the contemporary work of Sir Edwin Lutyens and C. F. A. Voysey.[9] The elaboration of the horizontal form, combined with its splayed plan, dominant low roof, Tudor half-timbering, banked leaded-glass windows, and tall chimneys had also been seen closer to home. Willis Polk, in his "Proposed Residence of Paul Foster, Esq., Suisun, California," was moving in this direction simultaneously with Wood and Simpson.[10] However, Polk's design did not approach the understanding of Lutyens and Voysey obvious in Hart Wood's presentation.

The turn to picturesque garden city principles, based on such English models as Gidea Park, Mill Hill, Port Sunlight, Hampstead Garden Suburb, and Woking, was perhaps in line with the artistic thoughts of both Wood and Simpson, but for both it was an abrupt change from the Beaux Arts planning of their previous work for Bliss and Faville and L. B. Dutton.[11] Wood and Simpson continued its investigation of garden city planning more pointedly in their design for a group of residences in Burlingame, located south of San Francisco on the peninsula. The town had incorporated in 1908 and had drawn an increasing number of commuting San Franciscans to its doorsteps by 1915. A regulated community with an emphasis on landscaping, Burlingame and its adjacent neighboring suburban communities of Hillsborough and Easton were exclusive places to live. The project's presentation sketch, signed "Hart Wood" and dated "15," illustrated a corner cluster of five moderately sized Tudor Revival houses surrounded by dense foliage. These houses were closer in theory and design to Gidea Park and Hampstead Garden Suburb than had been the Piedmont mansion (fig. 23).

Hart Wood and Horace G. Simpson executed distinctively different drawings for the Burlingame commission. Wood employed his penchant for flat, stylized background and framing foliage (usually eucalyptus or cypress) in his drawing, along with his viewer perspective well below the horizon. Rougher sketches accompanied the Wood presentation.

FIGURE 23. *Wood and Simpson, "A Group of Houses in Burlingame," watercolor published in* Architect and Engineer of California, *March 1916. Signed "Hart Wood" and dated "[19]15."*

Simpson initialed these drawings, numbering them and dating his group
of sketches September 1915.[12] Since the Wood houses and the Simpson
ones were not identical, the project included at least eight houses, if not
more. Real estate developers Lyon and Hoag of San Francisco may have
hired Wood and Simpson for the project. Lyon and Hoag were considering building a tract of residences in Burlingame, "following closely the
ideas of the English architects."[13] Such a proto–Tudor Revival group
would have been unusual in 1915–1916 in the Bay Area. The style,
although beginning to surface on both the East and West Coasts, was still
a rarity. Although the group of suburban houses remained unbuilt,[14] by
March 1916 Wood and Simpson had secured a paying residential commission.[15]

The Arthur Upham Pope and Phyllis Ackerman residence was a
house in two distinct parts, carefully designed to appear aesthetically
whole. The first unit was the Holt Manufacturing Pavilion, designed by
Horace G. Simpson while with Llewellyn B. Dutton.[16] Constructed for
the 1915 exposition in San Francisco, the pavilion was one of a select few
buildings purchased and moved for adaptive reuse following the close
of the fair (fig. 24).[17] Pope taught in the Philosophy Department at the
University of California at Berkeley and was renowned as an art historian
with expertise in Middle Eastern and Far Eastern textiles. His wife and
former student, Professor Phyllis Ackerman, was also an art historian,
one who specialized in European tapestries. Pope, a contemporary of
both Wood and Simpson, lectured in the Bay Area on aesthetics. He was
particularly fond of Japanese art and was instrumental in securing Phoebe
A. Hearst's rug collection for permanent loan to the San Francisco Art
Association at the Palace of Fine Arts.[18] A flatboat transported the Holt
Pavilion across the bay, and two Holt tractors hauled the building up the
steep Berkeley hills. Wood and Simpson redesigned the interior of the

FIGURE 24. *Horace G. Simpson, Holt Manufacturing Pavilion, Panama Pacific International Exposition, San Francisco, 1915. Photograph published in* Architect and Engineer of California, *May 1917.*

pavilion to meet the needs of a residence, adding the second unit in a continued Tudor style and giving the whole design a butterfly plan (fig. 25).[19]

Professors Pope and Ackerman's hiring of Wood and Simpson not only gave the new residence an artistic continuity with its original component, it also gave the young firm a chance to put some of their ideas on suburban housing into practice. Sited high in the hills, the house incorporated many of the principles put forth by Simpson during the preceding months in *Architect and Engineer of California*. The Pope-Ackerman

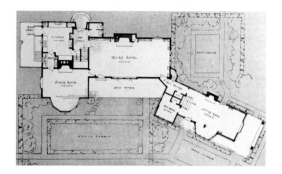

FIGURE 25. *Wood and Simpson, Pope-Ackerman residence, Berkeley, 1916. Floor Plan.*

residence reflected concepts of site design and vista that Hart Wood had used in his own house in Piedmont and demonstrated Wood's knowledge of native foliage and landscape. Contractors erected the house on two levels. Set close to one of the property lines, the house was angled on its site. Cultivated gardens included wildflowers to give rampages of color in both the spring and autumn.[20]

On the interior, the Pope-Ackerman residence displayed warmth and craftsmanship. The adapted Holt Pavilion was an almost archaeological, scaled-down interpretation of English Tudor architecture (fig. 26). The pavilion's main room had a low ceiling with exposed heavy beams, a floor of uneven narrow oak boards fastened with wooden pegs, and paneled walls of sandblasted spruce. The Holt Pavilion paneling was reminiscent of the sandblasted oak found in the additions to the St. Francis Hotel (1909). In both cases, the sandblasted paneling caught morning and evening sun, creating a feeling of warmth—a feeling further amplified in the Pope-Ackerman house by leaded-glass bay windows. A staircase opened directly onto the main room of the pavilion, also lending an accent of dramatic effect to the interior. Wood and Simpson adapted the second floor of the pavilion as a guest room and large attic studio.

In the angled addition to the Holt Pavilion, the architects continued a Tudor design for the Pope-Ackerman residence. The extension sat at a lower level, connected by a narrow passageway to the pavilion. Another, larger living room (fig. 27) offered more light-catching, sandblasted paneling. Pilasters separated built-in bookcases from each other and opened to reveal hidden shelving. Other details included a large fireplace. Plastered ceilings were low and flat, as well as high and arched. Three sides of the new living room offered views of the house gardens. In the east tym-

FIGURE 26. *Wood and Simpson, Pope-Ackerman residence, Berkeley, 1916. Exterior. (David Franzen, 1984.)*

panum wall, a reproduction of the Venus of the Sandal was recessed in a flat niche. The dining room (fig. 28) featured plastered wall treatment, as well as a fireplace, some sandblasted trim, and deep bay windows. The design of the 1916 wing may have been largely Hart Wood's. The clever pilaster panels with hidden shelves were reminiscent of the paneling in his own house of 1912, while the arched living room ceiling with recessed niche recalled his love of contrasting sculptural detail against stark planar wall surfaces.[21]

In November 1916, Wood and Simpson entered the competition for

FIGURE 27. Opposite. *Wood and Simpson, Pope-Ackerman residence, Berkeley, 1916. Holt Living Room. (David Franzen, 1984.)*

FIGURE 28. *Wood and Simpson, Pope-Ackerman residence, Berkeley, 1916. Addition of 1916, interior detail. Dining Room. (David Franzen, 1984.)*

SOUTH ELEVATION

FIGURE 29. *Wood and Simpson, design for the San Francisco State Building, 1916. Elevation of November 1916 published in the* Architect, *March 1917.*

the San Francisco State Building, a $1 million project. From the fifty-two entrants, the judges selected eight to participate in a second and final competition. Wood and Simpson were among the eight. In the distinguished company of Bliss and Faville, William C. Hayes, Bakewell and Brown, Charles Peter Weeks, Lewis P. Hobart, Loring P. Rixford, John Baur, and F. J. DeLongchamps, the firm must have felt both honored and frustrated. By mid-February 1917, the judges awarded Bliss and Faville first place, Charles Peter Weeks second place, Wood and Simpson third (fig. 29), and Bakewell and Brown fourth.[22] The competition hardly had closed, however, when controversy erupted. Outspoken Willis Polk made it well known that in his opinion Charles Peter Weeks should have been awarded first place, with Wood and Simpson second and Bakewell and Brown third. San Francisco architects quickly took sides. Edgar A. Mathews, William B. Faville, William Mooser, and George B. McDougall occupied one camp. Willis Polk, Arthur Brown Jr., George W. Kelham, Frederick H. Meyer, John Reid, Clarence Ward, and Charles Peter Weeks occupied the other. Wood and Simpson apparently stayed out of the fray. By June 1918, a revised committee had again decided the winner: Bliss and Faville.[23]

Similar to late 1915 and early 1916, the opening eight months of 1917 proved empty for Wood and Simpson. The surge of economic energy that had supported commissions for the Pope residence, the Randolph

Apartments, and the Santa Fe Building had quickly dissipated. Even a well-publicized exhibition of October 1916, held in Oakland and sponsored by the Alameda County Society of Architects, had failed to generate new projects for the firm.[24] Other architects illustrating their work in the East Bay show found themselves in a similarly bleak situation. As 1917 unfolded, alternatives became fewer still. At best, Wood and Simpson supervised the final construction phases of the Santa Fe Building and hoped that the controversy over the San Francisco State Building might resolve itself in their favor. The firm executed no published or exhibited studies, nor did it even have the bittersweet deflation of commissions fallen through. During this period, Horace G. Simpson became an editor for *Architect and Engineer of California.*[25]

In August 1917, Wood and Simpson finally landed work, with a commission to design fifty-five houses for the Pacific Electric Metals Company at Bay Point, California (east of Berkeley). The previous month, the Pacific Electric Metals Company had acquired tideland at the site. Their products were vital to the steel industry—an industry pressured by the demands of shipbuilding for the American war effort.[26] (The United States had entered World War I in April.) In addition to a group of concrete industrial structures, the Pacific Electric Metals Company commissioned a residential subdivision for its workers. The company awarded Wood and Simpson the contract for the subdivision, which the *San Francisco Chronicle* described as a "garden city for workmen." Residences were Tudor Revival, with overtones of Colonial, and the street layout was Olmstedian. The picturesque plan of the Pacific Electric Metals Company subdivision contrasted vividly with the remainder of Bay Point. The subdivision was sited near the only notable landscape feature in the town, a mature stand of eucalyptus trees.[27]

As had been true of the firm's suburban housing designs of 1915–

1916, Wood and Simpson's residential tract at Bay Point placed them on a cutting edge in the architectural profession. This project, along with such tracts as Goodyear Heights in Akron, Ohio (George H. Schwan), and Eclipse Park in Beloit, Wisconsin (George Post and Sons), was one of a very small number of war-related, single-industry villages built during 1916–1917. These enclaves both preceded and directly influenced what Lewis Mumford has recognized as the only substantial American efforts at garden city planning.[28] The Bay Point commission should have solidified the partnership of Hart Wood and Horace G. Simpson, but instead it was to be their final project together. As Wood and Simpson's largest commission and their only design noted in *American Architect*, Bay Point was too little too late.

With the conclusion of their second economically difficult year, in December 1917 the two men dissolved their partnership, each seeking his own way in a year that was to be even worse.[29] Simpson survived 1918 by designing a group of simplified Tudor houses for the Walter H. Leimert Company in Lakeside Highlands (Oakland).[30] Hart Wood, in contrast, faced a tougher set of circumstances. Although he did write a thoughtful essay on the housing crisis for the *Architect* in January 1918, illustrating his text with contemporary photographs from English garden suburbs, Wood did not design any additional suburban or industrial housing in the Bay Area. As the appropriations came through for the United States Shipping Board in February 1918, Hart Wood found himself working in a shipbuilding plant himself rather than designing the industry's housing. Many architects were doing the same, and Wood had a family with three young sons to support.[31]

During the fifteen months before Hart Wood left for Hawaii, the architect did undertake one commission that further expanded his endeavors in planned housing communities. In August 1918, he designed a group of farm buildings on Union Island (east of Berkeley) for William H. Metson. The Wood design for the Metson ranch was a fine one (although records indicate that the agricultural enclave remained unbuilt). Again evoking the aesthetics of Lutyens and Voysey, as well as the gardening and landscaping principles of McLaren, the U-plan ranch, with its attached tower and courtyard, would have been an unusual one for California—especially so for the conservative San Joaquin Delta.[32] Hart Wood showcased his drawings for the Metson project in an article written for the *Architect* in August 1918. He supplemented his design work for this essay with photographs directly borrowed from Alfred Hopkins' *Modern Farm Buildings*, a small book published in New York in 1913 and again in 1916.[33]

Architect Hopkins had designed a number of farm complexes in the northeast (notably on Long Island), all heavily photographed and reviewed for *American Architect* and *Architectural Record* during 1915 through 1918.[34] One of the most distinctive characteristics in Hopkins' designs was the organized layout of the farm. The individual buildings were "joined together by arbors and covered passages instead of being set down anywhere, without apparent relation, as on the ordinary farm." Hopkins' farms were generous in feeling. They were gentlemen farms—for businessmen with substantial other incomes. Hopkins' models, most appropriately, were the estates of England and Italy. Always arranged around three sides of a courtyard, with the fourth side left open, Hopkins' farmsteads contained a small cottage with attached carriage rooms, feed rooms, horse and cow barns, machinery and wagon rooms, and sheds. His farmstead was only one of the centers of interest on a farm. Large estates included a mansion, separate from the farmstead. For his Union Island ranch, Metson did not ask for a mansion or formal ranch house on the property. Listed in *Architect and Engineer of California* in September

1918, the ranch was a $15,000 job that featured wood-frame buildings with shingle roofs and rustic siding (fig. 30).[35]

The year 1918 was the worst of the 1914 to 1919 span. Professional journals repeatedly recommended that architects prepare for peace and use the empty months to overhaul their practices. Immediately following the armistice of November, the journals began predicting good years ahead.[36] Throughout 1918, Hart Wood did maintain an office in San Francisco, even though he was working in the shipbuilding plants.[37] Only one project had been initiated by his firm, the preliminary design for the Metson Ranch. Anxious and fatigued by the continued frustrations, architect Wood was ready for peacetime prosperity. In February 1919, *Architect and Engineer of California* noted that Hart Wood and Charles W. Dickey were in Honolulu reviewing upcoming projects for Dickey's firm. Dickey was one of the East Bay group of architects. The son of Hawaii's

FIGURE 30. *Hart Wood, design for the William H. Metson Ranch, Union Island, California, 1918. Drawing published in the* Architect, August 1918.

Senator Charles Henry Dickey, he had grown up in Honolulu and Oak-land.[38] Dickey had moved his architectural practice from Honolulu to Oakland in 1903 and had received his professional license in California in August 1904.[39] He was well recognized for his commercial and residential designs in Oakland and the surrounding area.[40] Hart Wood surely knew him, probably well. In April 1919, Dickey and Wood announced their partnership.[41] Wood was to handle the Honolulu office and Dickey the San Francisco–Oakland offices. Dickey had secured two residential commissions in Hawaii ($70,000 and $50,000) and the Castle & Cooke Building in Honolulu ($300,000). A forthcoming commission for the Bishop & Company Bank Building ($500,000) looked promising as well.[42]

As the partnership of Dickey and Wood began, Hart Wood could look back on twenty-one years of architectural practice in Denver and the San Francisco Bay Area. He had grown up in a building trades family focused on interior craft. His uncle was a frontier architect and his grandfather a carpenter. Hart Wood would become known for his attention to detail.[43] During the first seventeen and a half years of his professional life, he had worked for talented and recognized architects. In particular, his designs for Bliss and Faville had been of lasting quality. During the three and a half years of partnership with Horace G. Simpson and of independence, Wood had also made contributions—perhaps not recognized but nonetheless worthwhile—especially in the little-understood area of suburban and industrial housing. He had practiced during the very best of years (1911–1912) and during the very worst (1914–1918). And as Hart moved for the third time farther west, he must have wondered what lay ahead. The architect was thirty-eight.

HAWAII

THE STAGE IS SET

4 The pairing of Hart Wood (fig. 31) with Charles William Dickey (fig. 32) was to prove fortuitous for Wood. Dickey was able to provide Wood with the clients he had been unable to attract during the hard times of World War I. In turn, Dickey found in Wood a man of compatible architectural philosophies.

Dickey came from a family that had extensive connections in Hawaii's business community. This tightly knit community was almost exclusively comprised of Caucasian families whose roots went deep into nineteenth-century Hawaii. This elite controlled the "Big Five" companies: C. Brewer, Theo E. Davies Ltd., Castle & Cooke, American Factors, and Alexander & Baldwin. In turn, these firms controlled the sugar industry, which through World War II was the lifeblood of Hawaii's economy. Representing less than 20 percent of the population, this minority dominated the business, cultural, and political life of Hawaii.

Born in Alameda, California, Dickey was raised on Maui and was related to the influential Alexander family. He attended high school in Oakland and, after his architectural training at the Massachusetts Institute of Technology, had returned to Hawaii in 1896. Here he entered into practice with architect Clinton Briggs Ripley from 1896 to 1900 and with Edgar Allen Poe Newcomb from 1901 through 1904.

Hawaii's annexation in 1898 was followed by a six-year wave of building activity unmatched by any period in Hawaii's previous history.[1] The youthful Dickey rode the crest of this building boom exceptionally well, but by 1905 building activity was waning and he returned to California. He established his practice in San Francisco in 1905 after winning a school building competition in Oakland. His arrival roughly coincided with Hart Wood's appearance in San Francisco. During the next fourteen years, Dickey practiced in California but continued to do occasional work in Hawaii, most notably the Baldwin Memorial Church (1917) on Maui (fig. 33).

The effect of Hawaii's intense turn-of-the-century construction activity was substantial: Honolulu was virtually rebuilt following the lines of the Beaux Arts and Classical Revivals. Buildings, generally between two and four stories in height, frequently constructed of brick, dominated the streetscape (figs. 34 and 35). Local architects such as Oliver G. Traphagan, H. L. Kerr, Emory and Webb, and Ripley and Reynolds perpetuated these forms, whose appropriateness went virtually unquestioned until 1917 when Bertram Goodhue presented a series of drawings portraying Honolulu as a city of Mediterranean Revival style buildings (figs. 36 and 37). At the same time, Louis Mullgardt echoed similar thoughts in proposing a distinct Hawaiian Renaissance Revival form for downtown Honolulu, and Theo E. Davies & Company commissioned him to implement these ideas in their corporate headquarters (fig. 38).

This interest in establishing an appropriate regional architecture in Hawaii would blossom in the 1920s, thanks in large part to the nurturing hand of Hart Wood. The Bay Area architectural community of which Dickey and Wood had been members for many years had a strong self-

FIGURE 31. *Hart Wood, ca. 1920.*

FIGURE 32. *C. W. Dickey.*

FIGURE 33. *Baldwin Memorial Church,*
Maui, Hawaii. (Rick Regan, 1984.)

Above, Top to Bottom

FIGURE 34. *King and Fort Street intersection, ca. 1910. (Hawaii State Archives.)*

FIGURE 35. *Fort Street, Honolulu, ca. 1915. (Hawaii State Archives.)*

Above, Top to Bottom

FIGURE 36. *Sketch of Goodhue proposal for Honolulu.*

FIGURE 37. *Sketch of Goodhue proposal for Honolulu.*

conscious tradition of regionalism.
Wood's home in Piedmont testified
to his adherence to the tenets of
such thought. His encounter with
the dramatically new and different
environment of Hawaii surely must
have stirred his mind to think even
more along such lines.

In turn, Hawaii of the 1920s
was ready to support a self-defining
architectural form that emphasized
its climate and multiethnic heritage.
The Pan-Pacific movement, started by
Alexander Hume Ford immediately
prior to World War I, encouraged
people to view Hawaii as the "Cross-
Roads of the Pacific," where East met
West. Furthermore, the territory had
reached a period of adolescence:
When Queen Liliuokalani died in
1917, the most important symbol
of the overthrown monarchy also
disappeared. People in power could
feel secure that Hawaii was indeed an
American territory. No longer was it
necessary to emphasize the American
presence via architectural forms,
leaving builders free to develop a more
appropriate local architecture.

FIGURE 38. Opposite. *Theo
H. Davies Building, Honolulu,
c 1916. No longer extant.
(Hawaii State Archives.)*

The international temper of the times further accelerated the movement away from images of fiefdom to a distant government. The disillusioning aftermath of World War I and the ensuing brief economic depression may have led people to pull back and orient on a more local focus. Similar movements toward distinct regional design could be found in Canada, the American southwest, Florida, and California at this time. Also, in architecture, the Beaux Arts reliance on Renaissance and Classical forms was under attack: the Bauhaus movement proclaimed that a new era required a new design that embodied the spirit of the age. Rather than reject the past and take an international, global approach to the new age, regional architects found new impetus to explore forms that celebrated the historic continuity and character of their locations.

Hawaii had outgrown its tremendous preoccupation of identifying with the mainland United States, which had characterized its last building boom. By 1920 the island territory was growing both in population and economically, and it was proud of itself. By the beginning of the 1920s, Hawaii's population had risen 33 percent from 1910, to a total of 255,881. In the same period, Oahu's population had risen by an even faster rate, 51 percent, to a total of 123,496. This growth had been matched by the construction of housing but not by a corresponding increase in business and institutional buildings. These would come in the 1920s. By the end of the year 1921, it was clear that Hawaii had just gone through the greatest year of construction activity in its history. Throughout the decade, however, this record would be broken again and again.[2]

When Hart Wood moved into the Halekulani Hotel with his family in September 1919, the stage was set for the most creative and active period of his career.

EARLY
WORK
IN HAWAII

5 The basic designs of at least three major projects were completed before Wood made Honolulu a permanent base. The Greek Theater project, as its name implies, is pure Classical Revival architecture. However, the early schemes for the Bishop & Company Bank (fig. 39) and the Castle & Cooke Building (fig. 40) appear to conform with the Hawaiian Renaissance Revival forms Louis Mullgardt had proposed for Bishop Street, an early indication that Dickey and Wood already were thinking of Hawaii's architecture in a regional context. Of the three, only the Castle & Cooke Building was realized, and for reasons unknown, it displayed a solid Neoclassical Revival form (fig. 41).

These initial project designs all followed the strong Beaux Arts design path that was well established during Wood's career at Bliss and Faville. Other early designs done in Hawaii—the W. E. Bogardus residence and the Clarence Cooke Swimming Pool—similarly employed Classical styles, as did the later Likelike School.

By August 11, 1920, the rough concrete work for the Cooke's pool and bathing pavilion (fig. 42), a scaled-down version of the proposed facade of the Greek Theater project, was completed. This $15,000 project incorporated an 18-by-40-foot pool into a landscaped area of

FIGURE 39. *Bishop Bank Building sketch, 1919.*

FIGURE 40. *Castle & Cooke Building sketch, ca. 1919.*

FIGURE 41. *Castle & Cooke Building,*
Honolulu, ca. 1920. No longer extant.

FIGURE 42. *Cooke Pool Pavilion, Honolulu, ca. 1920. (Bishop Museum photo.)*

150 by 100 feet, which was part of the extensive grounds owned by the Cooke family in lush Nuuanu Valley. The project is significant for at least two reasons: its strong Classical Revival style and its landscaped setting.

The latter demonstrated Wood's continued interest in landscape design. His early experiences with Frank Edbrooke and Marean & Norton in Denver had influenced his sensitivity to landscape design, but—with the exception of the Pan-Pacific International Exposition—he had been given little opportunity to engage this interest during his years with

Bliss and Faville. In Hawaii, Wood's interest in the landscape setting of his buildings was to blossom into a major element of his work.

The $21,000 Classical Revival Bogardus residence was completed about the same time as the Clarence Cooke Swimming Pool. The Bogardus residence is a symmetrically arranged two-story home with a gabled roof and pediments over the main entry and dormers on the front (fig. 43). The front entry is framed by an elliptical fanlight and sidelights, and the interiors continue this Classical detailing and layout (fig. 44).

In spite of its adherence to Colonial Revival principles, two characteristics of the home show some awareness of local building traditions. The symmetry of the house is affected by the presence of a twelve-foot wide lanai, similar to a mainland sunporch. The lanai runs across the entire leeward, sunny side of the house and away from the driving rains of the valley.

The second characteristic is the presence of latticework between the columns of the entry, with each panel embellished with a wreath (fig. 45). The lattice may have been installed to provide some wind and weather protection for the entry. Latticework was usually associated with screening for crawl spaces in vernacular dwellings in Hawaii. However, a precedent also existed in the Islands for its use in lieu of solid walls, allowing maximum ventilation and a degree of privacy. Wood would have been familiar with this usage in at least the Catholic Church in Waikiki and King Kalakaua's bungalow on the grounds of Iolani Palace, if not also in a host of luau halls situated at various rural churches. The feeling of lightness and airiness imparted by the use of the latticework would be repeated in other projects throughout Wood's career, further accentuating an entry porch's mediatory role between indoors and out. The use of lattice shows an early interest in motifs appropriate to Hawaii's balmy climate. Wood's reliance on Beaux Arts forms quickly diminished, and Likelike School (1923) was his last major project to adhere to Neoclassical thought.

FIGURE 43. *Bogardus residence, Honolulu. (David Franzen, 1983.)*

FIGURE 44. Opposite. *Bogardus residence front entry, Honolulu. (David Franzen, 1983.)*

As the construction of the Bogardus residence and Cooke Swimming Pool were nearing completion, another of Wood's commissions was
rising on Alewa Heights, overlooking Honolulu. The earliest mention of
the Herman Von Holt residence in newspapers was an announcement
that plans had been completed for a home that was to be "Italian in style."
The article called the house "something out of the ordinary, apart from

FIGURE 45. *Bogardus residence,
Honolulu, interior stair. (David
Franzen, 1983.)*

the usual in design" (figs. 46–49). This Mediterranean-influenced style was a relatively new form in Hawaii, but one that was embraced with increasing frequency in the ensuing decade.[1]

Construction of the $16,000 home was begun in September 1920, and it was completed by the end of May 1921. The home, though only one story, appears much larger from a distance because it sits on a terraced platform that adds to its bulk. Lava rock rubble excavated from the site was used to construct all the terrace and house walls. The stone was embedded by placing it into the fresh concrete as its twenty-inch-thick walls were poured.

FIGURE 46. *Herman Von Holt residence, exterior, ca. 1922.*

FIGURE 47. *Herman Von Holt residence living room. (David Franzen, 1983.)*

FIGURE 48. *Herman Von Holt residence. (David Franzen, 1983.)*

FIGURE 49. *Herman Von Holt residence. (David Franzen, 1983.)*

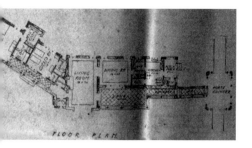

FIGURE 50. *Francis Ii Brown residence.*

The design of the Von Holt house was not only a new style for Hawaii, it was a new residential style for Hart Wood as well. Until this time he had worked almost solely in English Tudor Revival styles, consistent with his interest in English garden suburbs. Although he had not previously used the Spanish Mission style, he must have had some familiarity with it from his exposure to California examples. Wood, always conscious of siting and of selecting the appropriate design for the site, no doubt felt this style to be perfect for the property. Early photographs show the home sitting on a dry, rocky site that could have been transplanted from the southwestern United States.

As construction on the Von Holt residence progressed, Mr. and Mrs. Francis Ii Brown liked what Wood had designed for their friends, the Von Holts, and immediately commissioned him to design a similarly styled but larger residence for them.[2] To be constructed on Pacific Heights, a ridge on the opposite side of Nuuanu Valley from Alewa Heights, the $25,000 house was constructed of stuccoed masonry with a tile roof. A single depth of rooms was placed adjacent to an open loggia, which, combined with the high ceilings of the residence, improved the natural ventilation of the home (figs. 50–51).

FIGURE 51. *Francis Ii Brown residence.*

A sketch of the house first appeared in the January 26, 1921, *Star-Bulletin* in an article calling the residence "typically Hawaiian" in style. In discussing this house with reporters, Hart Wood articulated his thoughts on the potential development of a regional architecture in Hawaii:

> Several attempts have been made to create a Hawaiian Style but styles in architecture aren't created—they grow—and the way one style runs into another is by adapting an existing style to meet the needs and peculiarities of a certain climate or location.
>
> A Hawaiian style would have to be adapted from styles already in existence in countries where the climate is similar. One would not expect to find a style in England or a northern European country to be used here. One would have far more reason to expect a good prototype from the southern countries and for that reason the buildings of Spain, Italy, the southern United States, Mexico and Central American countries would answer the requirements met here. They would be easily adaptable to this climate.[3]

Wood went on to say that in developing a Hawaiian style of building, the use of wood should be eliminated wherever possible due to the attacks of termites.

It is significant that this home was publicized as typically Hawaiian when only a few months before the newspapers referred to the similar Von Holt home as "unusual." This is an obvious attempt by Wood to get publicity and to transplant some of his ideas about regionalism to Hawaii. By the end of 1920, after little more than a year in Hawaii, Hart Wood was beginning his search for an architecture suited for the Islands. The next few years would see him exploring different forms and materials in

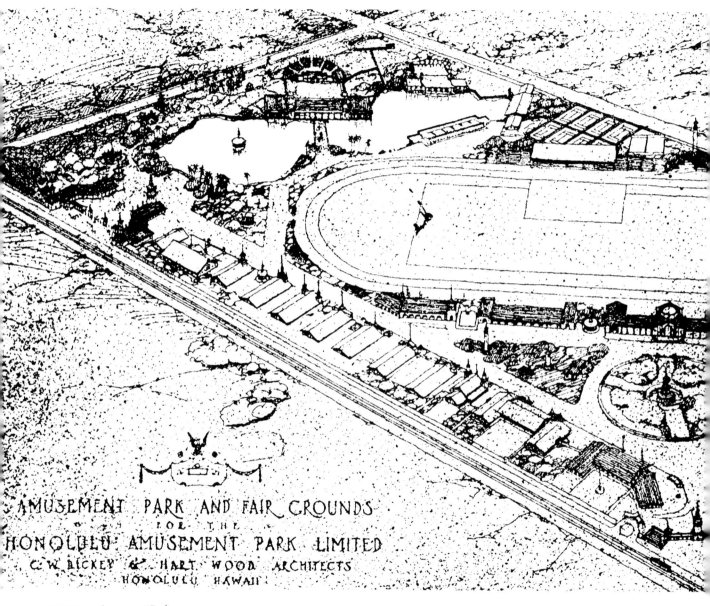

AMUSEMENT PARK AND FAIR GROUNDS
FOR THE
HONOLULU AMUSEMENT PARK LIMITED
C. W. DICKEY & HART WOOD ARCHITECTS
HONOLULU HAWAII

FIGURE 52. *Amusement Park and Fair Grounds, sketch by Hart Wood.*

this search, and in a short time "Hawaiian style architecture" would be buzzwords in Hawaii's building industry.[4]

A little more than one year after settling in Hawaii, Wood's partnership with Dickey ended. In a September 22, 1920, article with the heading, "Probabilities Are Honolulu Will Lose Architect C. W. Dickey," reference was made to the fact that Dickey would not be able to return to Honolulu due to the extensive Oakland school building program for which he had been retained.[5] The article concludes with the statement, "Hart Wood is comparatively new in the islands but has become acquainted with many people who feel that he will manage well in his own canoe." Wood was essentially on his own, although the contacts he made through Dickey would continue to serve him well.

For Hart Wood, 1921 began with a project proposal that was never built. On February 9, the drawing of a ninety-acre amusement park in the Moiliili area was unveiled for a Hawaii Territorial Senate committee hearing.[6] The park included a swimming pool and boat course, a polo field/racetrack, a bathhouse, playground, dining area, outdoor theater, merry-go-round, scenic railway, and—significantly—an Oriental Village and a Hawaiian Village. At the opposite end of the park was a territorial fair section for a large number of commercial and farm exhibitors (fig. 52). Unfortunately, the legislators decided not to fund this project. However, the proposal served as a public announcement of Hart Wood's willingness to dedicate his talents to enhance the quality of life in Hawaii.

In 1921, Wood had several projects on the island of Kauai: the Wilcox Memorial Library in Lihue, the Wilcox Memorial Parish Hall, and the restoration of the 1837 Waioli Mission House and 1841 Mission Hall. His initial contact with the island was certainly through Dickey, who was the grandson of William P. Alexander, the first pastor of Waioli Mission. Dickey's architectural contact with the island went back to at least 1903, when he designed a home in Lihue for Mr. and Mrs. Ralph Wilcox, members of another powerful Kauai family that owned both Grove Farm and Lihue Plantations.

Wood's exposure to the Waioli buildings almost certainly affected his design work on the other two Kauai projects, as well as his subsequent work. Waioli Mission Hall (fig. 53) was constructed in 1839–1841 as a replacement for an earlier church of Hawaiian thatch construction. It is often cited as an example of the early combination of Hawaiian and Western building methods. The huge shingled roof duplicates the pitch and shape of the earlier thatch structures, but its materials and trussing derive from Western traditions, as also do the building's walls, windows, and lanai. The lime plaster over rough-hewn wood stud walls are dwarfed by the roof, the building's dominant visual element. The roof over the interior space is steeply pitched but changes to a lower pitch for the portion of the roof over the lanai, which wraps around the church, adding a second visual dimension to the building.

During the restoration, Wood did extensive work on the roof, replacing structural elements and adding tie beams above the ceiling to eliminate the bowing of the walls. He also replaced flooring and roof shingles and added a small, inconspicuously located toilet-room facility to one corner of the church. His handling of the restoration and addition showed great sensitivity to the historic nature of the Mission Hall.

In contrast to the Mission Hall, the neighboring Mission House was a New England saltbox and looked like it had been lifted from the homelands of its Protestant missionary builders. The difference between this transplanted style and the vernacular form of the church was to have an immediate effect on Wood.

The Parish Hall in Lihue (figs. 54 and 55) was under construction by December 1921. It owes a clear debt to the Waioli Mission Hall. Its enor-

FIGURE 53. *Waioli Mission Hall.*
(Augie Salbosa Photography, 1993.)

FIGURE 54. *Lihue Union Church Parish Hall, Lihue, Kauai, Hawaii, 1922. Collection of Justin Tomita, Honolulu.*

FIGURE 55. *Lihue Union Church Parish Hall, Lihue, Kauai, Hawaii. (David Franzen, 1983.)*

mous double-pitched gable roof, deep lanai, and prominent columns all quote the Mission Hall. In addition to experimenting with the building form, Wood used local lava rock in a short but prominently located bell tower that was embellished with concrete detailing in a Beaux Arts style and cast-iron pieces garnered from sugar plantation machinery. Thus the architect further expanded his concept of regional architecture in terms of materials and motifs.

The incorporation of such forms in the Parish Hall discloses a new direction in Wood's search for an appropriate architecture for Hawaii. Rather than define "typically Hawaiian" architecture in terms of a transplanted historical Western style appropriate to warm climates, as in the Brown and Von Holt residences, Wood attempted in the Parish Hall to define an appropriate regional design in terms of Hawaii's distinctive historical antecedents. The Parish Hall builds on the forms that earlier generations seemingly developed unconsciously in response to their situation.

The Wilcox Memorial Library (figs. 56 and 57) combines Beaux Arts classicism with rustic local materials used in a new way in Hawaii. It reflects Wood's encounters with Kauai's vernacular buildings at Waioli and also his consciousness of the emerging civic center in Lihue. This was Kauai's first library building and one of Lihue's first substantial buildings. In 1921, Lihue was a relatively new town, designed with wide streets to accommodate automobiles and laid out in a traditional manner, with a civic center surrounded by business districts. The only substantial structures in the town were the County Building (fig. 58), the Plantation Store, and the Bank of Hawaii Building. These buildings were Classic Revival in style and had set the tone for Lihue.

The library is a bold combination of Neoclassical elements and new design ideas that bridge two stylistic worlds. The Beaux Arts design of the entry may be viewed as an attempt to address the Classical designs of the

FIGURE 56. *Wilcox Memorial library, Lihue, Kauai, Hawaii, front facade. (David Franzen, 1983.)*

FIGURE 57. *Wilcox Memorial library, Lihue, Kauai, Hawaii, side and rear elevations. (David Franzen, 1983.)*

FIGURE 58. *Kauai County Building.*

other buildings of the civic center area. In contrast to the entry facade, the remaining elevations are strikingly different. Once again a large, steeply pitched roof is a dominant characteristic of the building. The manner in which local lava rock is incorporated into the building was also important. Until this building and the Parish Hall were constructed, lava rock had been primarily used two ways in construction. As early as the late 1880s, a very dense lava rock had been quarried into blocks and used for rusticated stone masonry, usually in Romanesque Revival buildings. A more porous, weathered uncut lava rock had also been used in vernacular housing, usually in foundations and porch columns, although C. W.

Dickey had used it in 1917 as a veneer on the Makawao Union Church. Wood transformed the porous, weathered, uncut lava rock into a primary building material, evocative of the Islands that it created.

Hart Wood used the native lava rock in a new, distinctive way in the library and exalted it as a major design element. Although the rear elevation is somewhat awkwardly designed, the combination of rubble coursing with concrete window trims, water table, and string courses was very successful. This experimentation with local materials was an important continuation of Hart Wood's early work in Hawaii and accentuated the possibilities of employing local stone as a building material.

Hart Wood's fourth son and last child, Donald, was born in 1922. During that year, Wood was awarded the commission to design the Likelike School Building. The plans of the building were completed by August 9, 1922, and the building itself was dedicated on February 3, 1923. This building, which cost $97,200, was a large commission for Wood. It consisted of a two-story center structure with single-story wings on each side, the walls built of reinforced concrete, with a steeply pitched, wood-framed and -shingled roof over the main two-story section (fig. 59).

Likelike School shows a strong Beaux Arts influence and presents a

FIGURE 59. *Likelike School, Honolulu. Drawing from* Honolulu Advertiser, *February 3, 1923. No longer extant.*

conservative countenance. The design may be a reflection of its institutional nature, but its massing and details hark back to Wood's early design roots. The one element that stands out as inconsistent with this design past is the handling of the roof, which is monumental in scale with deep overhangs. It is instructive to compare this building with two others being built at the same time: McKinley High School (fig. 60) by Davis and Fishbourne and the Federal Building by York and Sawyer (fig. 61). Both these buildings are stylistically consistent Spanish or Mediterranean forms with virtually no overhangs and with roof lines that are not nearly as dominant. In contrast, the Likelike School's roofline and general detailing are more similar to two school buildings designed by C. W. Dickey: the slightly Mediterranean Kaiulani school (ca. 1900) and the grander Bishop Hall, done by Dickey and Newcomb in 1901 (fig. 62).

FIGURE 60. *McKinley High School, Davis and Fishbourne, Honolulu. (Augie Salbosa, 1981.)*

FIGURE 61. *Federal Building and Post Office, York and Sawyer, Honolulu.*

FIGURE 62. *Bishop Hall, Punahou School, Honolulu, by C. W. Dickey, 1901. No longer extant.*

Following his work on Kauai, a short article, "Have Islands Real Architectural Type, Is Question Raised" appeared in the *Honolulu Star-Bulletin* on July 26, 1922. It provided further insight into Wood's thinking about regional architecture.

What is the real type of modern Hawaiian architecture? This is a question that Hart Wood, local architect, says is difficult, if not impossible to answer. Probably the broad lanai with overhanging eaves is the thing that is more distinctive of island homes than any other single characteristic. . . .

Hart Wood calls attention to the fact that the several sections of Honolulu are vastly different in climate and environment and that a type of architecture that would be exactly the thing for one locality would be sadly inappropriate in another.

. . . The setting and surroundings of the home together with its furniture have as much to do with its possessing a character purely Hawaiian or island, as anything else.

Natural Hawaiian volcanic stone such as is found in Kaimuki offers an excellent building material that has high artistic value if properly handled . . . according to Hart Wood. He states that beautiful effects in large and pretentious homes could be obtained from this rock.[7]

The article concludes with a prediction: "For the man who can develop a distinctive as well as appropriate type of architecture for Hawaii, there lies a large future, in the opinion of Hart Wood." That man, by implication, was to be Hart Wood himself.

The design of the First Church of Christ Scientist (fig. 63), the major project in Wood's office in 1923, continued his search for a distinctly Hawaiian style. Wood was an active member of the church throughout

his life in Hawaii. Wood was born into the Methodist religion and reared
as a Lutheran. He joined the Christian Science Church while living in
San Francisco, as a result of a visit by a proponent of Mary Baker Eddy's
teachings who was canvassing the neighborhood.

Construction of the coursed rubble walls of the First Church of
Christ Scientist was already well underway by mid-year, and it opened
for its first services on December 30, 1923. As with most of Wood's
projects, placement of the building on the site was carefully considered
and became an important part of the viewer's perception of the building:
"Set back in spacious grounds under large, overspreading trees its unique
architecture presents a picturesque appearance."[8]

Wood's willingness to draw from various sources for inspiration and
to unify these sources into a cohesive whole was clearly demonstrated
in this building (fig. 64). The concrete Gothic motifs found in the entry
and the pinnacle convey a sense of the sacred, announcing to all that this

FIGURE 64. *First Church of Christ Scientist, Honolulu. Collection of Justin Tomita, Honolulu.*

is a holy place. The interior is a simple, high volume with large rusticated wood beams reflecting a Tudor Revival, Arts and Crafts influence. The prominent screen in the chancel (fig. 65) was inspired by Madonna della Seggiola in Ravenna, Italy. Wood claimed to have spent more time detailing the screen than he spent designing the entire building.

The Gothic/Arts and Crafts influences were combined with several other elements to give the church a distinctly Hawaiian flavor. Newspaper accounts referred to the fact that only local materials were used in its construction. This is an overstatement. However, the use of stained concrete for the floors and the coursed lava rock walls represented distinctly local materials or uses of materials. The steep roof with wide overhanging eaves and the deeply recessed lanai with mortared rubble columns were other elements previously used by Wood that symbolically tied the building to Hawaii. The use of the side lanai to open the building was a major contribution made by Wood to ecclesiastical design in Hawaii (fig. 66).[9]

From 1920 through 1924, Wood also designed a number of individual homes, among them the Bosworth residence, the Home Electric or Dr. Nathaniel Benyas residence, the George R. Ward residence, and the Bukeley and Butler residences. The 1920 design for the Bosworth residence was a modest home that Wood noted was "of southern colonial design." The facade is dominated by a fourteen-by-twenty-five-foot lanai. Wood made a point of mentioning that the Bosworth residence was "one of a number of standardized types of moderate-priced homes upon which the firm has been recently engaged, following an insistent demand upon it for distinctive drawings at comparatively reasonable figures."[10]

FIGURE 65. *First Church of Christ Scientist, interior, Honolulu. (Augie Salbosa, 1981.)*

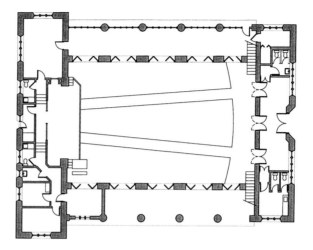

FIGURE 66. *First Church of Christ Scientist, floor plan.*

FIRST CHURCH OF CHRIST SCIENTIST

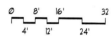

Wood continued to explore the possibility of reasonably priced housing in his plans for the Home Electric, which were completed in November 1920. This house was designed as a demonstration of modern living, the way people in Hawaii would be living in the electric age. Although the house has some Colonial Revival detailing, it has a completely asymmetric plan and elevation. The main entry into the house is through a large lanai, and the house is longitudinally organized to maximize natural ventilation (fig. 67). As was Wood's custom, the home was prominently sited, and the front appeared more imposing because the floor is raised about four feet higher than the front yard.

The design of the house was a tremendous success. During the three days it was opened to the public in mid-May 1921, approximately 1,500 people visited the home. With an $11,330 price tag, the house was not

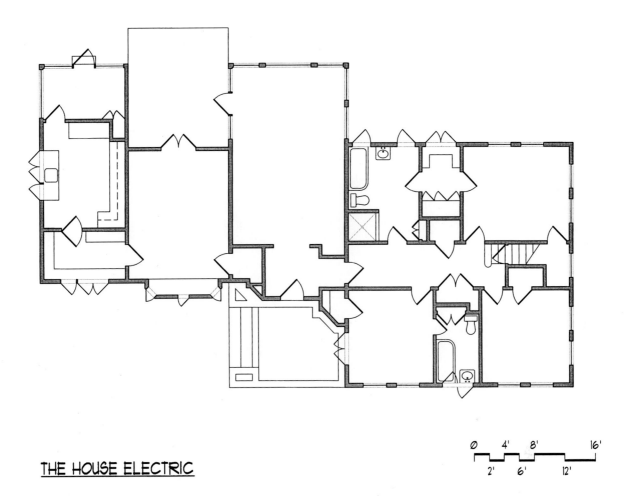

THE HOUSE ELECTRIC

exactly moderately priced because at that time a nice home could be
had for $5,000–$6,000. Still, it was designed with moderate incomes in
mind. The Ward residence (fig. 68), located a mere block away, appears
to have been a spin-off of this concise house. Built in 1924, this dwelling
also employed an informal Colonial style and featured a prominent entry
lanai, leading the *Star-Bulletin* to describe it as "one of the most attractive
residences recently completed in Honolulu."[11]

FIGURE 67. *House Electric, floor
plan.*

FIGURE 68. *Ward residence, Honolulu.*
(Augie Salbosa, 1981.)

Early in 1922, prior to the completion of the Wilcox Memorial Library in May, design work on the Bukeley and Butler residences was completed. These two residences were commissioned by Rudolph Bukeley, the latter for his mother-in-law, Mrs. Florence Butler. The houses sat on adjacent lots in Manoa Valley and were demolished in the 1970s. The $15,000 Bukeley residence was the larger of the two, but both shared common design elements. Both were wood framed with large, steep roofs that changed pitch at the eaves (fig. 69).[12]

The Bukeley house was one and a half stories in height, with limited fenestration on the windward side, providing some protection from the Manoa rains. The leeward side was very open, providing views of the city and horizon. From the entrance on the windward side, an unobstructed view of Diamond Head could be seen through the living room, which opened onto a covered lanai. The dining room also opened onto a covered lanai, which was protected by a lattice screen on one side. The two lanais were connected by a large grassed terrace.

In the Bukeley and Butler residences, Wood continued his earlier advocacy of the Tudor style as the embodiment of home, but now he modified this style and combined it with forms from Hawaii's past. An eclectic mixture of borrowed and traditional elements melded into one form, these houses further reveal Wood's attempt to develop distinct designs appropriate to the Islands.

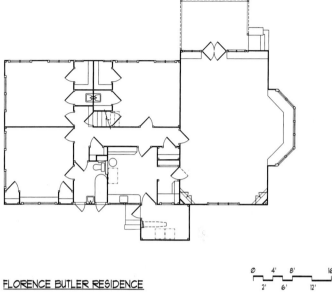

FLORENCE BUTLER RESIDENCE

FIGURE 69. *Butler residence.*

WOOD LEADS THE HAWAIIAN REGIONAL ARCHITECTURE MOVEMENT

6

During the years 1924–1926, Wood continued to combine a variety of design elements in an effort to formulate the guiding principles for a regional architecture appropriate to Hawaii. The directions he had explored in the Albert Wilcox Memorial Library, Wilcox Memorial Parish Hall, First Church of Christ Scientist, and the residences of Francis Ii Brown and Rudolph Bukeley were perpetuated and further developed in five residential commissions of this period. The houses built for attorney and later territorial governor Ingram M. Stainback and for Doctors Van Poole, Morgan, Reppun, and Faus represent the work of a mature designer combining traditional elements in new ways that teeter on the cutting edge of a new architectural conceptualization of Hawaii. Each of these houses eclectically embodies a variety of forms, in an attempt to create a new architecture appropriate for the Islands. They vividly reflect Hart Wood's thoughts of the moment:

> We often hear, that Hawaii should have a distinctive style of architecture for her homes, but those who make the statement seldom realize that the development of an architectural style is not a matter of accomplishment by one generation. It takes hundreds of years to establish an

accepted "style"—and then it will be, in all probability, a combination
of several other "styles," molded to the especial requirements of a local
condition.[1]

Five completely different design concepts, these residences disclose
the variety of avenues pursued by Wood once the thought of Hawaiian
Regionalism crystallized in his mind. Distinct statements unto themselves, each house stands as an initial step, the foundation stone on which
the architect and others might build more mature designs.

The most elaborate of the houses, the Dr. James A. Morgan residence, dwells primarily within the stylistic lines of the Mediterranean
Revival with its tile roof, round arched openings, and lava rock walls
covered with plaster (figs. 70–72). Built in "the rambling Spanish style,"[2]

FIGURE 70. *Morgan residence, Honolulu. Exterior in 1920s.*

the residence's sprawling plan maximizes the opportunities for cross-
ventilation and provides multiple vistas of its verdant grounds. A glo-
rification of its lush, temperate setting, the house well reflects Wood's
heightened awareness of Hawaii's beneficent climate and resonates
with the architect's love of quality detail (figs. 73–80). An open second-
floor passageway provides the only connection between the bedroom
wing and stairway to the first floor, requiring the residents to regularly
encounter the outdoors on their daily sojourns between bedroom and
the world. Similarly, the dining room opens, through sliding doors, onto
lanai on two sides and a paved courtyard on the third.

FIGURE 71. Opposite. *Morgan residence, Honolulu. (David Franzen, 1981.)*

FIGURE 72. *Morgan residence, Honolulu. (David Franzen, 1981.)*

FIGURE 73. Opposite. *Morgan residence, Honolulu. Living room. (David Franzen, 1981.)*

FIGURE 74. Above. *Morgan residence, Honolulu. Dining room. (David Franzen, 1981.)*

FIGURE 75. Left. *Morgan residence, Honolulu. Water feature sculpture seen from dining room. (David Franzen, 1981.)*

FIGURE 76. *Morgan residence,
Honolulu. Interior column detail,
the work of Mario Valdestri.
(David Franzen, 1981.)*

FIGURE 77. *Morgan residence,
Honolulu. Lanai details. (David
Franzen, 1981.)*

FIGURE 78. Opposite. *Morgan
residence, Honolulu. Main
stairway. (David Franzen, 1981.)*

FIGURE 79. Opposite. *Morgan residence, Honolulu. Second floor hallway detail. (David Franzen, 1981.)*

FIGURE 80. *Morgan residence, Honolulu. Chapel. (David Franzen, 1981.)*

The Dr. Gideon M. Van Poole residence stands as an uneasy dialogue interlaced with Colonial and Mediterranean Revival quotations (figs. 81–88). Sited above Nuuanu Stream on a beautifully landscaped lot, this house further explores the possibilities of recombining traditional architectural forms to create a new three-dimensional statement on Hawaii's heritage and climate. The gable-roofed second story stirs Colonial associations, while the stuccoed first story and its cloister walk with vaulted ceilings and round-arched openings bespeak a Mediterranean and Renaissance influence. An amazingly adroit essay in juxtaposition, the dwelling's formal living room and large, more casual, enclosed lanai at the rear of the house open on each other and a Classically inspired terrace, overlooking the less formally planted, more tropical Nuuanu Stream. Like the Morgan residence and so much of Hart Wood's work, this substantial house, which cost approximately $25,000 to build in 1924, is beautifully detailed throughout. Wood's sensitive handling of materials and attention to detail gave him a reputation in Honolulu's cultural circles as an artist of enormous talent.[3]

FIGURE 81. *Van Poole residence, Honolulu. Rear lawn opening to Nuuanu Stream. (David Franzen, 1983.)*

FIGURE 83. *Van Poole residence, Honolulu. Entry vestibule. (David Franzen, 1983.)*

FIGURE 82. Opposite. *Van Poole residence, Honolulu. (David Franzen, 1983.)*

FIGURE 84. *Van Poole residence, Honolulu. Entry. (David Franzen, 1983.)*

FIGURE 85. *Van Poole residence, Honolulu. Custom light fixture. (David Franzen, 1983.)*

FIGURE 86. *Van Poole residence, Honolulu. Note the use of wood paneling, rusticated cased opening to stair, and art glass. (David Franzen, 1983.)*

FIGURE 87. *Van Poole residence, Honolulu. Living room. (David Franzen, 1983.)*

FIGURE 88. *Van Poole residence,*
Honolulu. Rear enclosed lanai.
(David Franzen, 1983.)

FIGURE 89. *Stainback residence, Honolulu.*
(Augie Salbosa, 1981.)

The more modest Dr. Carl Reppun and Ingram M. Stainback residences both incorporate local lava rock as a primary design element, albeit in a more straightforward, fieldstone pattern rather than the dramatic
string coursing of the First Church of Christ Scientist. The Stainback
residence includes a lattice entry porch, enhancing a person's awareness
of the entry functioning as a transitional space. This dwelling also has a
spacious open-beam living room ceiling, a feature the architect frequently
employed to invoke a sense of comfortable domesticity (figs. 89 and 90).

FIGURE 90. *Stainback residence,
Honolulu. (Augie Salbosa,
1981.)*

FIGURE 91. *Reppun residence. (Augie Salbosa, 1981.)*

In contrast to the ground-hugging horizontality of the Stainback residence with its prominent gable roof and flared eaves, the Reppun residence thrusts upward from a large terrace sculpted from the steep Ewa (west) slope of Manoa Valley. Essentially a foursquare without a porch, the austerity of this dwelling's concrete first story was initially mitigated by vines, an unsuccessful attempt by Wood to better integrate house and landscape (fig. 91).

The Dr. Robert Faus residence was completed in June 1924 (figs. 92–95). From the front the house appears to harken back to Wood's mainland years, as this single-story, Elizabethan Tudor Revival building, complete with rolled eaves and half-timbered walls, presents itself to the street. Located on a steep site that drops to the rear, the house, when viewed from the back, reveals itself to be three stories in height, with "an English basement, where dining room and kitchen are located."[4] On this elevation the walls utilize the same coursed masonry that Wood used at the First Church of Christ Scientist and the Wilcox Memorial Library. The architect would use this patterning only one more time, in the Kapiolani Park Bandstand of 1926 (fig. 96).

The coursed lava rock masonry of the bandstand's sides backframed the stage while giving its round-arched proscenium a solid foundation. In the 1930s a conical roof, supported by two tall columns, was added to better protect the stage from the elements.

The interiors of the Faus residence are simple, with fiberboard paneling on the walls and ceiling. The dining room light fixtures, which Wood designed, are distinctive because of their Asian detail. In all likelihood the incorporation of this detail and also the pair of Chinese columns in the Morgan residence were the result of Wood's working on the design of the Mrs. Charles M. Cooke residence in the spring of 1924.

FIGURE 92. *Faus residence, Honolulu. Front or street elevation. (Augie Salbosa, 1981.)*

FIGURE 93. *Faus residence, Honolulu. Rear elevation. (Augie Salbosa, 1981.)*

FIGURE 94. *Faus residence, Honolulu. Entry hall. (Augie Salbosa, 1981.)*

FIGURE 95. *Faus residence,
Honolulu. Custom light fixture.
(Augie Salbosa, 1981.)*

FIGURE 96. *Kapiolani Park
Bandstand.*

FIGURE 97. *Anna Rice Cooke
residence, Honolulu. Sketch by
Hart Wood.*

The Cooke commission signaled a new direction in Hart Wood's work and ushered in a new era, which would result in some of his finest projects. An amalgam of Chinese and Western elements, the Mrs. C. M. Cooke residence (figs. 97–101) was "unusual and almost unique in its style derivation."[5] Through the sensitive incorporation of Chinese decorative elements into a Western massing, Wood developed a distinct and distinguished design "in the Chinese manner." The Chinese columns framing the entry, the teak pillars supporting the courtyard's lanai roof, and the masonry grills and wood railings that follow geometric Chinese patterns all helped to convey an Asian sensibility. Also, the roof was made of tile, "in accurate imitation of the sun-baked black mud tiles of China, and the dip in the roofline is characteristic."[6]

The inspiration for this exquisite design derived from Mrs. Cooke's grand interest in Chinese art and furniture. The house was constructed to showcase much of her collection. For many years, Mrs. Cooke had been a major patron of the arts in Hawaii, and the need to build this house was a result of the donation of her home on Beretania Street opposite Thomas Square as the site of the soon to be erected Honolulu Academy of Art, which was designed by Bertram Goodhue.

Mrs. Cooke was instrumental in nurturing a sensibility for Chinese art in Hawaii, and she frequently patronized the establishment of Yuen Kwock Fong Inn at the corner of Pauahi Street and Nuuanu Avenue in Honolulu. In the years immediately before World War I, Mrs. Cooke encouraged this koa furniture maker to expand his commercial enterprise to include the importation of Chinese objets d'art and furniture. As a result, his store became a focal point for Chinese art within Honolulu, and Hart Wood was one of many customers to gain an enhanced sensibility for the aesthetics of Asia from Fong Inn.

An interest in Hawaii as the "Crossroads of the Pacific" was in the

FIGURE 98. *Anna Rice Cooke residence, Honolulu. Collection of Justin Tomita, Honolulu.*

FIGURE 99. *Anna Rice Cooke residence, Honolulu. Collection of Justin Tomita, Honolulu.*

FIGURE 100. *Anna Rice Cooke residence, Honolulu. (Augie Salbosa, 1982.)*

FIGURE 101. *Anna Rice Cooke residence, Honolulu. (Augie Salbosa, 1982.)*

air via the recently reenergized Pan-Pacific Movement, and this further supported the emerging infatuation with Chinese and, later, Japanese art forms. As early as 1908, the Reverend E. W. Thwing, in a lengthy letter to the editor of the *Pacific Commercial Advertiser*, noted the potential of Honolulu to support a general museum that exhibited both Eastern and Western art.[7] Lectures such as those given in the spring of 1911 by Philip H. Dodge, following his return from a four-year stay in Japan, further fostered an appreciation for Asian art in Hawaii.

For someone who had never been to Asia, the blending of Chinese and Western forms must have been a challenging task. Wood had to undertake a major research and learning process to discover the special vocabulary of Chinese forms. Throughout and following the Cooke commission, Wood continually built up his repertoire of motifs, garnering inspiration from pieces of art and furniture owned by Mrs. Cooke, the painter Thomas Bartlett, Helen Kimball's Curio Shop, the Honolulu Academy of Arts, and Fong Inn and from such books as the following: Leigh Ashton's *An Introduction to the Study of Chinese Sculpture* (London: Ernest Benn Ltd., 1924); Osvald Siren's *The Walls and Gates of Peking* (London, 1924), *Chinese Paintings in American Collections* (Brussels: G. Van Orst, 1928), and his three-volume set, *The Imperial Palaces of Peking* (Paris and Brussels: G. Van Orst, 1926); Ernst Boerschmann's two-volume portfolio, *Chinesische Architektur* (Berlin: E. Wasmuth, 1925); Laurence Binyon's *The Eumorfopoulos Collection of Chinese Frescoes* (London: Ernest Benn Ltd., 1927); and Kazumasa Ogawa's two-volume portfolio, *Photographs of Palace Buildings of Peking* (Imperial Museum of Tokyo, 1906), and his *Report of the Imperial Museum of Tokyo on the Decoration of Palace Buildings, Peking* (Tokyo, 1906), as well as other more obscure places.[8] Wood's sketchbook reveals a variety of sources from which he borrowed details and gained a feel for Chinese

proportion, rhythm, and design (figs. 102 and 103). Designs garnered
from such diverse objects as a cabinet at the Academy of Arts, a vase
at the Bartlett residence, and a chair from Fong Inn later would be
incorporated into his architecture.

The surface was Wood's prime concern. He was an artisan of high
quality working with the embellishment of building surfaces, and the
manipulation of space appears to have been of secondary importance
to him. Such a facility to employ ornamentation to convey ideology
allowed him to move easily and expertly into Asian motifs. Once he had
established a vocabulary that he could employ, he was on his way. Once
a motif appeared in his work, there was a high probability that it would
reappear.

The design of the Mrs. C. M. Cooke residence in 1924, with its
introduction of Chinese motifs, concluded a five-year quest by Wood
for architectural elements appropriate to Hawaii. He had come to terms
with the Islands and had developed the vocabulary that he would use
for the next three decades to define Hawaii in three-dimensional terms.
The need to address climatic concerns, the eclectic intermingling of traditional motifs with each other, the use of local materials, attention to
ornamentation in general and especially to elements deriving from Asia, a
sensitivity to the landscape, and a willingness to work toward developing
quality, moderately priced housing became the primary theoretical pre-
occupations that would guide Wood's work.

From this point onward, Hart Wood would define Hawaiian architecture as a mixture of the tropics with Hawaiian, New England, and
Asian influences, or as he stated in 1931,

> Architecture is as much a creature of precedent and tradition as law. We
> may think for a while that tradition and precedent are both being defied,

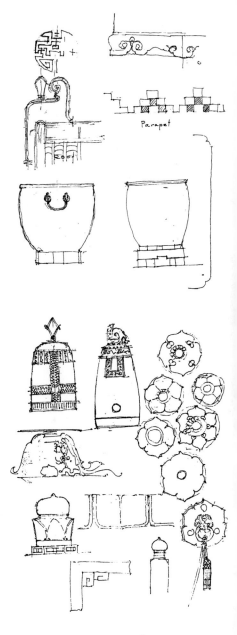

FIGURES 102 AND 103. *Pages
from Hart Wood's sketchbook,
showing many details later
included in some form in the
1929 A & B building.*

but we see in time that attempts at defiance are short lived, or that what we thought defiance was merely tradition in a new or strange guise.

In Hawaii, architectural history scarcely furnishes sufficient background for tradition or precedent. We have, it is true, a few distinctive roof lines, the heritage of the almost negligible architectural efforts of the Hawaiians. Then there is Kawaiahao Church, the product of home taught builders, working with strange materials in an alien land, under the handicap of exceedingly primitive circumstances. Nevertheless, it is a type which bespeaks the inspiration of consecrated devotion to unselfish service.

It is simple, rugged, sincere, unostentatious, dignified and straight forward. It is devoid of any architectural sophistication and is the embodiment of most of the characteristics connected by the word "Hawaiian" as applied to architecture. It is a type of a certain group of buildings erected during the early years of the "Haole" (white) settlement, which were built about the same time and under similar conditions, which we recognize as embodying in a general way those qualities which make them "belong" which we refer to more or less loosely as "Hawaiian" and which were the natural outgrowth and expression of the conditions from which they grew.

In the last half-century or so, the introduction of a strong Oriental element into the population brought another influence, which although disdained by its own of the second generation for some of the more modern if less distinguished styles of their adopted land, is nevertheless exerting a decided and increasing influence on the more serious work of the Islands.

Such buildings as the new Alexander & Baldwin Building, the Honolulu Academy of Art, the new building of S. and G. Gump and the residences of Mrs. C. M. Cooke and Mrs. Robert C. Pew show an unmistakable trend toward the expression of this newer, but numerically predominant element. So what is lacking in tradition bids fair to be supplied by borrowed sources.[9]

The merging of Chinese motifs and Western forms in the Cooke residence provided Wood with much acclaim, both in Hawaii and the mainland. The renown of this residence led to similar but larger commissions in the ensuing years. As a result, a fascination with integrating Eastern elements into the architectural idiom of Hawaii dominates Wood's work for the next five years. This fruitful period saw the production of some of Wood's finest designs, including the S. and G. Gump Building, the Chinese Christian Church, the Alexander & Baldwin Building, the Henry Inn Apartments, and the Mrs. Nellie Pew residence.

Alice Spalding Bowen commissioned Wood in 1927 to design the Honolulu branch of S. and G. Gump of San Francisco (figs. 104–107). Constructed in Waikiki, across the street from the recently completed Royal Hawaiian Hotel, the store catered to the affluent traveler and the upper stratosphere of Honolulu society, who were justly proud of the fact that Hawaii had a Gumps before Los Angeles. Featuring an outstanding collection of antiques, jewelry, and objets d'art from both Europe and Asia, the store was labeled "a treasure house in the Pacific," and upon its opening in February 1929, the newspapers acclaimed it as the "latest addition to the art life of Honolulu."[10]

The building reinforced the refined, high-culture image of its occupant and clientele and at the same time maintained the noncommercial air that Mrs. Bowen had nurtured in her own house/studio since 1923, when she first began to represent the Gumps in Hawaii. From the start, everyone involved in the project "shared the determination to make this a unique building, more like a residence than a place of business."[11] Following

FIGURE 104. *Gumps Building, Waikiki. (Hawaii State Archives.)*

FIGURE 105. Opposite. *Gumps Building entrance, Waikiki. (Hawaii State Archives.)*

FIGURE 106. Opposite. *Gumps Building showing grille, second floor lanai, and window design. (Hawaii State Archives.)*

FIGURE 107. *Gumps Building moon gate to side garden. (Hawaii State Archives.)*

the introduction of Gump's houselike appearance, other Honolulu buildings—most notably, C. Brewer's corporate headquarters—were designed
in a similar vein, as were several Waikiki establishments such as the
Green Lantern restaurant. The possibility that the Gump Building influenced the design of C. Brewer is high. In July 1928, Hardie Phillip, the
New York architect who designed the C. Brewer Building, wrote to Hart
Wood, "Harry Bent sent me a newspaper clipping which describes quite
completely the building you are designing for S and G Gump Company.
The project sounds terribly interesting, and I should think one which
would give you a great deal of fun. Looking forward with keen interest to
seeing it the next time I come out."[12]

In response, Wood wrote to Phillip, "I saw the perspective of the
new Brewer building reproduced in yesterday evening's paper and I want
to congratulate you. It looks remarkably good and seems to have to an
unusual degree that quality which, without knowing what it is, we call
Hawaiian."[13]

A blend of Mediterranean and Chinese forms, set back from the
street by a landscaped lawn, the two-story, $75,000 S. and G. Gump
Building "carried out the Oriental theme and at the same time was
harmonious with the type of architecture most desirable to Hawaii."
Through the design and construction of this building, Wood seems to
have further reflected on the definition of an appropriate regional architecture for Hawaii. Moving beyond forms, Wood now began to place his
work within a new rhetorical context, as an "expression of friendly charm,
hospitality, spaciousness and comfort which is expected in the more
'Hawaiian' buildings, whether in Spanish, Italian, English or Oriental
style."[14] For Wood, such intangible characteristics, which many modern architects might be hard pressed to ascribe to their own creations,
became the goal of any so-called Hawaiian style of architecture.

Moving beyond the Hawaiian style of the new building, the complimentary commentary of the newspapers enthusiastically emphasized the building's artistry, analyzing it as if it were a painting. Perceptions of the structure, perhaps influenced by the architect, revealed the building in terms of its color, texture, and setting, without becoming enmeshed with stylistic elaborations. Although each room was described, no mention was made of the flow or handling of space or the relationship of the parts to the whole. Instead, attention was directed to the contrast between Gump's oyster-white stucco walls and its imperial-blue roof tiles, and how this contrast was softened by the green verde antique copper gutters, leaders, and leader heads. The landscaped setback from the street and the courtyards were also mentioned, but the store's relationship to the distant landscape was found to be even more compelling, as the building and its backdrop of a "clear blue sky and the cloud banked tapestry of the Koʻolau mountains presents a picture of rare color values."

Attention was also given to the appropriate and novel use of materials: The entry and balcony railings of Burmese teak, "stained a rich reddish brown black so characteristic of the better types of Chinese furniture," introduced a sharp contrast of color; tatami mats made at Kyoto's Imai Shoten covered the Oriental hall's floors; ceilings were made of rough concrete, with form marks left exposed and treated with naphtha stains and dry colors; the Spanish room's ceiling was of weathered, antique gray wood; the acid-stained concrete floors featured amber, jade, and terra-cotta colors; and ingrain carpeting with nap side out covered the walls of the second-floor painting gallery. Detail by detail, the description devoutly developed an overall impression that architecture was without a doubt one of the seven fine arts, and Hart Wood, a master artist, had carefully brought forth a remarkable work of art worthy of housing other works of art.

Four months after the opening of the Gump's store, on June 16, 1929, "one of the most artistic churches in Honolulu," the Chinese Christian Church on King Street, was dedicated. This commission, the result of an open architectural competition in which six to eight architects participated, brought further acclaim to Hart Wood's artistic talents and his genius for working in a Chinese mode (figs. 108–111).

The design met the requirements of the competition in that it expressed the Chinese heritage of its congregation and also met "orthodox Christian needs." Dominated by a pagoda-inspired bell tower, the church featured a basilican floor plan with an inset lanai appended to either side of the nave. As in the First Church of Christ Scientist, these lanais provided illumination, ventilation, and supplemental side aisle access. Besides the obvious Chinese-flavored elements of the facade and roof, a variety of ornamental details, including the stained glass windows, the fretwork in the choir loft railing, the light fixtures, and the use of masonry grillwork, further reinforced the Chinese associations of the

FIGURE 108. *Hart Wood at the Royal Hawaiian, ca. 1927, shortly after it opened.*

building. Surrounded by gardens, the $65,000 church stood not only as another tangible example of the juncture of East and West in Hawaii but also as a celebration of the lushness of the Islands.[15]

The crowning achievement of Wood's efforts to intermingle East and West can be found in the Alexander & Baldwin (A & B) Building. Erected as a corporate headquarters and memorial to the founders of the company, the project's generous budget was an architect's dream come true. Meticulously detailed, the 52,000-square-foot building cost $1,241,947 to build—approximately $22 per square foot in a time when a modest commercial building could be erected for $4 to $8 per square foot.

C. W. Dickey, a grandson of the company's founder, Samuel T. Alexander, undoubtedly procured the commission. Dickey had returned to Honolulu in 1925, and in 1926 the partnership of Dickey and Wood had been resumed. However, the two architects appear to have worked independently of each other on separate projects, although they shared the same office and firm name.[16] Thus, while Wood busied himself with the S. and G. Gump Building, the Chinese Christian Church, and a number of residential commissions, Dickey was at work on the cottages for the Halekulani Hotel, the Girls Industrial Reform School, and the Kona Inn. Why the two men collaborated on the Alexander & Baldwin Building is unknown, but that they did cannot be regretted. The building stands as one of the masterworks of architecture in Honolulu, epitomizing the so-called Hawaiian style of design.

On February 29, 1924, Alexander & Baldwin's board of directors decided to purchase land on which to erect a headquarters building and memorial to its founders, Samuel T. Alexander and Henry Perrine Baldwin. By 1926, the company had acquired the block-long frontage on Bishop Street, the heart of Honolulu's financial district. Initial drawings for the building were prepared and revealed a Classical facade comparable to

FIGURE 109. *Sketch of the Chinese Christian Church. Collection of Justin Tomita, Honolulu.*

FIGURE 110. *Front elevation of Chinese Christian Church.*

Dickey and Wood's earlier design for the Castle & Cooke Building, which neighbored the A & B lot on the mauka side. However, by November of 1926, preliminary plans show a shift in style, favoring a more richly ornamented, Asian-influenced facade (figs. 112–117). Over the next two years this plan was considerably modified, with the current form not approved until May 1, 1928, five months after the start of construction.

The four-story building (figs. 118–122) was considered completely fireproof, as no wood was used in its construction. It has a structural steel skeleton that supports the terra-cotta walls and a tile, double-pitched (Hawaiian style) roof. The facade's symmetry focuses on the thirty-five-foot-high, inset, centered portico. This strong vertical element is tempered by a fourth-story loggia that runs the length of the facade and the overhanging eaves of the roof with their exposed rafters.

While the basic form and massing of the building derived from Western traditions and is attributable to Dickey, the extensive yet subtle embellishment drew its inspiration from Asia and was largely the work of Hart Wood, although Mr. Trapet of Gladding, McBean terra cotta company should be credited with the ornamental tile work of the entry porch.[17] Upon the official opening of the building on September 30, 1929, C. W. Dickey gave Hart Wood credit for his help in developing the design of the building and went on to explain the ideas underlying the design:

> My foremost thought architecturally was to produce a building suit-
> able to the climate, environment, history and geographical position of
> Hawaii. The early history of the sugar industry, upon which the firm of

FIGURE 111. *Interior of Chinese Christian Church.*

·STUDY· f⁼ ·ALEXANDER· & ·BALDWIN· BLDG·
C·W· DICKEY — ARCHITECT — MAY 5, 1926

FIGURES 112–117. *Various sketches of the Alexander & Baldwin (A & B) Building, Honolulu, illustrating the design evolution.*

BUILDING FOR
ALEXANDER & BALDWIN LIMITED
DICKEY & WOOD, ARCHTS. HONOLULU

Alexander & Baldwin Ltd., was founded, was most closely linked with Chinese labor. It was felt that this, added to the location of Honolulu as the crossroads of the Pacific, in close touch with the Orient, gave sufficient reason for allowing Chinese architecture to clearly influence the design.

Once adopted, this idea led to fascinating results. It was found that the wide projecting roofs and balconies of China, as well as the deep window reveals of some of the fine stone structures of old Peking, were admirably adapted both artistically and practically to a building in Honolulu. It was also found that there was a wealth of Chinese architectural details that could be used without becoming blatantly Chinese.

The problem naturally was to design an appropriate modern building to fit modern needs and yet feel the Chinese influence without making it appear that the building itself, or any part of it, was transplanted from China. To obtain this result required great self-restraint, and literally hundreds of sketches were discarded as being too strongly Chinese in flavor, and I feel that in the final building the exotic Chinese influence is so subtle that it would not be noted by a casual observer. However, it is there in every detail of the design. On the exterior it is most pronounced in the water buffalo heads and quaint Chinese faces of the window ornamentation, in the circular "Good Luck" signs at the main entrance portico on Bishop Street and the long life signs in the column capitals.

An interesting point in this connection is that many of the elements of the ornament, such as wave patterns, egg and dart, lamb's tongue,

FIGURE 118. *Overall view of A & B Building, Honolulu.*

FIGURE 120. *A & B Building, Honolulu. Front entry. (Augie Salbosa, 1981.)*

FIGURE 121. *A & B Building, Honolulu. Detail at entry doors. (Augie Salbosa, 1981.)*

FIGURE 119. Opposite. *A & B Building, Honolulu. Detail of bronze windows and terra-cotta exterior at windows. (Augie Salbosa, 1981.)*

etc., that occur so frequently in Classical architecture are found in a somewhat modified form throughout the architecture of the old buildings of the Imperial City of Peking, and this ornament in its Chinese form is used in the Alexander & Baldwin Building.

The art tile work of the main entrance portico surrounding the panels of Hawaiian fish life is all carried out in Chinese motifs, as are the acoustical tile of the ceiling of the big room on the first floor and the decoration of the ceiling beams.

The influence of Chinese art is strongly felt in the fretwork and ornament of the bronze grilles for doors, windows, elevator fronts, elevator cars, balustrades, etc. and in the inlaid floors of black Belgian marble and Roman travertine stone in the public space in front of the main counter on the first floor.[18]

As Dickey's discussion reveals, the building was a myriad of decorative details—certainly Hart Wood at his most exuberant height. Wood's revelry of exquisite detail, color, and craftsmanship repeatedly astounds the viewer, so that even the newspaper noted, "Architectural and artistic details of the building have been worked out with the greatest of care, and only repeated visits to the structure will reveal the many intricate details that have been worked together to make the building an harmonious whole."

A masterful composition, the building was a striking addition to Bishop Street, the premier address in the downtown area.[19] Dickey and Wood's masterpiece took its place opposite Louis Mullgardt's Theo H. Davies Building and a block down from Bertram Goodhue's Bank of Hawaii, and it became the fourth Big Five corporate headquarters on the street. Standing across Merchant Street from the Neoclassical Castle & Cooke Building, it well revealed how far Hart Wood—and in turn, the architecture of Honolulu—had moved in less than a decade.

FIGURE 122. Opposite. *A & B Building, Honolulu. Original lobby. (Hawaii State Archives, 1981.)*

To further accentuate the new building's presence, and "to create a tropical setting," it was set back from the sidewalk with a landscaped space. Honolulu's pioneer landscape architect, Richard Tongg, was responsible for the rather straightforward landscape design, and the mature coconut palms that appeared along the street overnight came from the former Kapiolani Maternity Home site, the gift of C. R. Frazier. This project was the first to landscape a commercial building in downtown Honolulu and reflected Wood's thinking on the integral relationship of a building and its setting. For a final touch, the Bishop Street sidewalk was stained green, utilizing Robert Lammens' recently perfected Keramik staining process. The newspapers were, of course, quick to note how the cool green sidewalk artistically harmonized with the tan terracotta walls.

Differences concerning the administration of the A & B project led to the dissociation of the apparently already tenuous partnership of Dickey and Wood in the spring of 1928. On February 20, 1928, Wood provided Dickey with a ninety-day notice of dissolution of the partnership:

Dear Will:

Since it has become evident to both of us that it is not possible to reconcile our different ideas of the best methods of conducting the practice of architecture and that it will be to our mutual advantage to henceforth go our separate ways in a professional sense—so in keeping with the terms of our agreement providing for such a contingency, I take this means of complying with the provision therein made and request that this be considered as the ninety day notice and that we arrange to conduct our professional and business affairs separately from a period of ninety days hence, or earlier if we can come to an arrangement mutually satisfactory. This I do with great reluctance because of our very satisfactory relations of the past several years and of the high esteem in which I hold you.

I wish to take this opportunity to acknowledge your many acts of generosity and helpfulness. If, under the stress connected with the conduct of a large amount of work under somewhat difficult circumstances, I have seemed at times to be forgetful of appreciation please believe that I never the less retain a deep sense of your fine qualities and generous nature.

With very keen regrets for the disappointment of our hopes and with the very best wishes for your future success, I remain

Sincerely your friend,

Hart Wood[20]

The final parting of ways transpired sometime before June 1, 1928. The A & B Building was a masterful combination of the two men's talents, and its complete inspiration can be claimed by neither. Opening on the eve of the depression, it marked a high point in both men's careers, both in terms of its magnitude and its quality of design. In the separate careers that ensued, neither would design a better building.

In Wood's post–A & B oeuvre, Asian elements would appear at times in his work but would again figure prominently only in the Mrs. Nellie Pew residence on the slopes of Diamond Head and the Henry Inn Apartments, both of which date from 1931. The Pew residence (figs. 123–130) introduced a Japanese gable roofline into a Chinese-Western composition of moon gates, lanai, courtyard, and blue tile roofs. The mood of the house was set by the serenity of its front courtyard and lanai. The exterior repose was perpetuated on the interior, as the enormous expanse of the living room contrasted with an intimate dining room entered via a moon gate opening and an equally intimate, wood-paneled mezzanine library.

Wood's meticulous attention to detail, via the use of wrought iron and Asian decorative elements, further contributed to the subtle atmosphere that pervaded the house.

The Henry Inn Apartments on Seaside Avenue in Waikiki, which included a two-story apartment building with five duplex cottages behind it, opened in August 1931. The *Honolulu Advertiser* found the apartment house to be "different from any before seen in Honolulu," embracing "the old world and the new in design and treatment." The newspaper went on to blithely declare the complex "The First Apartment House of Its Kind in the World." Hip gabled roofs with upturned corners bestowed an Asian character upon the buildings, which was dramatically augmented by the

FIGURE 123. *Pew residence. Sketch by Hart Wood. Collection of Justin Tomita, Honolulu.*

RESIDENCE FOR MRS NELLIE C PEW
HART WOOD ARCHITECT

FIGURE 124. *Pew residence, Honolulu. (Augie Salbosa, 1981.)*

FIGURE 126. *Pew residence, Honolulu. Lanai. (Augie Salbosa, 1981.)*

FIGURE 125. Opposite. *Pew residence, Honolulu. Entry court. (Augie Salbosa, 1981.)*

FIGURE 127. *Pew residence,*
Honolulu. Living room. (Augie
Salbosa, 1981.)

FIGURE 128. *Pew residence, Honolulu. Library. (Augie Salbosa, 1981.)*

FIGURE 129. *Pew residence, Honolulu. View to lanai. (Augie Salbosa, 1981.)*

FIGURE 130. Opposite. *Pew residence, Honolulu. Dining room. (Augie Salbosa, 1981.)*

FIGURE 131. *Dr. Carey Miller residence, Honolulu. (Augie Salbosa, 1981.)*

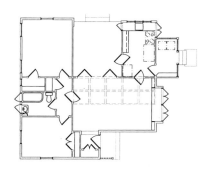

DR. C. MILLER RES.

FIGURE 132. *Dr. Carey Miller plan.*

incorporation of antique Chinese decorations, all imported by Fong Inn, within the design program. The windows in the bungalows, as well as much of the main building, came from "ancient Chinese mansions," and camphor wood dragons, teak fu dogs, Chinese terra-cotta, and fretwork abounded. The apartment interiors were well ventilated, as sliding panels opened the top half of an interior wall to allow the free flow of air between the bedroom and living room. Within weeks all the units were rented, a silent testimonial to "the beauty, comfort and charm of these apartments."[21]

Besides incorporating Asian motifs in his major works, Wood acknowledged Hawaii's cosmopolitan culture in several smaller residences as well. Such commissions as those for University of Hawaii home

FIGURE 133. *Dr. Carey Miller residence.*
Living room. (Augie Salbosa, 1981.)

FIGURE 134. *Front door to the Harold Mountain residence. (Augie Salbosa, 1981.)*

economics professor Carey Miller (1924) and Castle & Cooke official Harold Mountain (1937) could easily pass on the exterior as standard tract housing. However, on the interior these modest single-wall dwellings reveal Wood's hand with their high level of craftsmanship, open-beam ceilings, multilevel floors, indoor-outdoor relationships, and subtle use of Asian elements.

Nestled in Manoa Valley, the board-and-batten, L-shaped Miller cottage (figs. 131–133) is surprisingly spacious, with its wood-paneled living room running the length of the lateral wing. The well-conceived plan includes a Dutch door that opens on an inset rear lanai that serves as an outdoor dining area. Bamboo is utilized to detail this space in a manner reminiscent of Japanese use of this material.

The Harold Mountain residence, a dozen years later, similarly employs bamboo in its entry gate and exterior covered walk, which leads to a central courtyard (figs. 134 and 135). As with the Chinese columns in the Dr. Morgan residence and the dining room light fixtures in the Tudor style Dr. Faus residence, the use of such solitary Eastern elements in an otherwise Western context could be viewed as incongruous. Yet within the social and architectural milieu of Hawaii, the combination resulted in a harmonious whole, conveying a message that such a casual mix was indeed merely an extension of everyday life, a demonstration of the enriching symbiosis of East meeting West.

Western idioms, as embodied in period revival houses, also remained a large part of Wood's work during the period 1926–1931. Mediterranean forms continued to appear in his residential work, most

FIGURE 135. *Interior of the Harold Mountain residence. (Augie Salbosa, 1981.)*

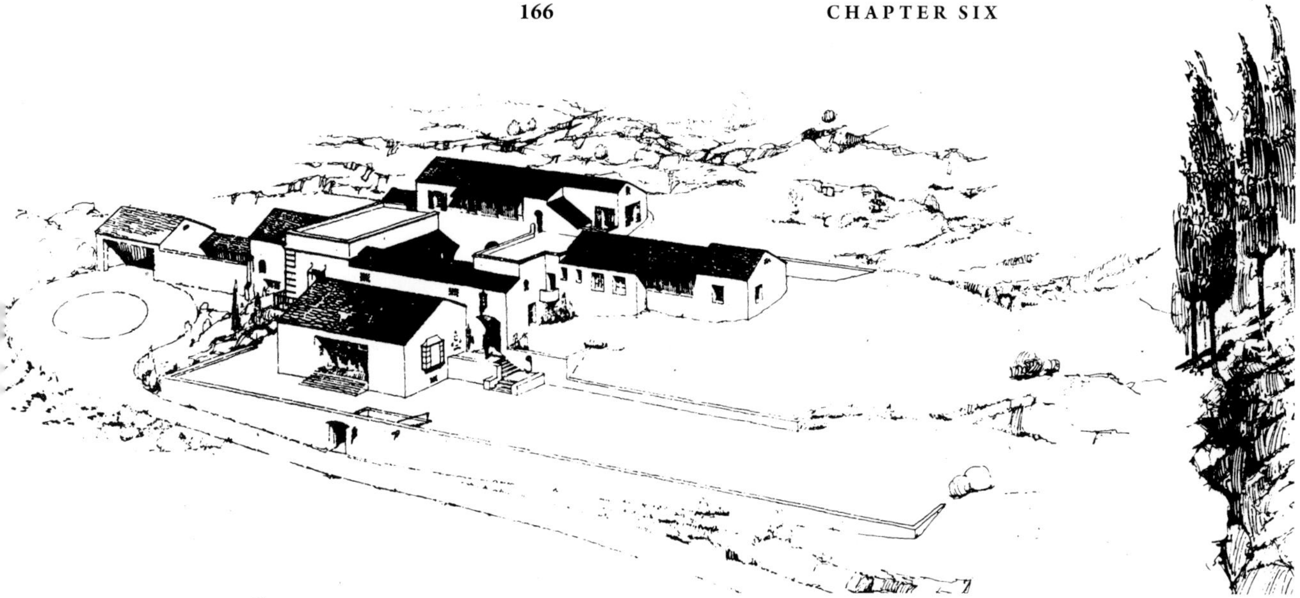

FIGURE 136. *Canavarro residence, Honolulu. Sketch by Hart Wood. Collection of Justin Tomita, Honolulu.*

notably Georges Canavarro's residence on the slopes of Nuuanu Valley and the Paul Winslow residence on Pacific Heights, which were completed in 1927 and 1928, respectively. The $61,000, 6,710-square-foot Canavarro residence (figs. 136–140) was described as being "of Sicilian type architecture, and to Elmer Garnsey, world traveler and artist, is reminiscent of some of the finest work he has seen in Sicily."[22] Situated on a sloping site, the house is laid out on four levels around a diminutive central courtyard with a fountain of Tunisian tile at one end. Like so many of Wood's residences, it is a masterpiece of high-quality detail with its painted ceilings and ornamental light fixtures, the product of B. B. Bell of Los Angeles. Although situated at a sufficiently high level in the valley to afford a fine view of the city, the house is remarkable in that the only vista it provides is from the master bedroom suite's loggia. Both the dining and living rooms, as well as the courtyard, focus on themselves and their entertainments rather than the diverting outside world.

Perched on Pacific Heights, the Paul Winslow residence (fig. 141),

completed in 1928, enjoys magnificent vistas of the city from its rooms
and lanai. Built for the manager of the Moana Hotel, this house presents
an engaging Tudoresque massing garbed in Spanish Mission Revival
materials, while maintaining a flowing openness of the Islands in its
primary spaces. The red tile floors of the dining room step down to a
capacious living room, which expands outward onto a large rear lanai.
The openness of the public areas contrasts with the more intimately
designed second-story bedrooms, which were originally accessed by
a circular stairway off the rounded entry hall. Hart Wood ordered red
terra-cotta shingle tiles from the Heinz Roofing Company in Denver to

FIGURE 137. *Canavarro residence shortly after construction. Collection of Justin Tomita, Honolulu.*

FIGURE 138. *Canavarro residence. (David Franzen, 1981.)*

roof the building. As a matter of economy, he laid the pieces broken in shipping in an inch of lean mortar with half-inch joints to add character to an otherwise mundane tar and gravel, flat garage roof. Louis Mullgardt would later deliberately make such materials to roof the Taylor residence in Berkeley. [23]

In addition to these two residences, Wood was also involved in several Spanish Mission–style public buildings. Spanish forms became the predominant governmental style in Hawaii during the 1920s and 1930s,

FIGURE 139. *Canavarro residence.*

FIGURE 140. *Canavarro
residence. Living room.
Collection of Justin Tomita,
Honolulu.*

FIGURE 141. Opposite. *Paul
Winslow residence, Honolulu, ca.
1930. (Hawaii State Archives.)*

with fire stations, schools, post offices, police stations, libraries, mental hospitals, territorial office buildings, and city halls dotting the landscape with cream stucco walls and red tile roofs.[24]

Honolulu's City Hall, Honolulu Hale, was a joint venture utilizing the firms of Rothwell, Kangeter & Lester, Robert Miller, and Dickey and Wood (figs. 142 and 143). An imposing pile of stuccoed masonry, its commanding eight-story corner tower and three massive bronze portals provide strong statements for public respect, if not awe and civic pride. Completed in 1927, the $750,000 building centers on a majestic court-yard—an impeccably detailed, ninety-foot-square, fifty-five-foot-high space with tiled floors and hand-painted ceilings. The building's design was a combined effort, with the more engineering-oriented Guy Roth-well named as the supervising architect for the project. Dickey and Wood appear to have been instrumental in the decorative detailing, Wood's forte. Such details as the wrought iron light fixtures—including the courtyard's chandeliers and sconces—the cast stone grillwork, the main entry, and the tower balcony were all drawn by Wood.[25] In addition, S. Peterson of Los Angeles, who was responsible for the execution of much of the decorative work in the Alexander & Baldwin Building, was hired to paint the ceilings of the entry and courtyard.[26]

In comparison to Honolulu's ebullient City Hall, the Wood-designed Territorial Office Building in Lihue is a most modest structure (fig. 144). Constructed of reinforced concrete at a cost of $33,420, this 1930 building is essentially a rectangular, eighty-nine by forty-six-foot box with a red tile hip roof. Offices are stacked on either side of a central corridor, and a pair of Doric columns and decorative masonry grilles provide the only embellishment.

The residence of Dr. Paul Withington, a close friend of the Wood family who influenced the architect to send his two eldest sons to Har-

FIGURE 142. *City Hall,*
Honolulu. (Augie Salbosa.)

FIGURE 143. *City Hall. Central courtyard. (Augie Salbosa, 1981.)*

vard, started as an open, earth-hugging, Mediterranean villa (fig. 145).
However, by its completion in 1926, the house had morphed into a
distinctly Tudor design with its steep-pitched roof, prominent, diamond-
paned central bay window, and splendid living room (figs. 146–148). The
house focuses on the baronial living room, a grand hearth-oriented space
embellished with an open-beam ceiling, massive fireplace, wrought iron
fixtures, and heavy timberwork in the mezzanine and doors. A medieval

FIGURE 144. *Kauai County
Annex Building, Lihue, Kauai.*

FIGURE 145. *Withington residence, Honolulu. Sketch signed by Wood on January 1, 1931. Collection of Justin Tomita, Honolulu.*

FIGURE 146. *Withington residence under construction. Collection of Justin Tomita, Honolulu.*

FIGURE 148. *Withington residence. Back lanai with sleeping porch above. Collection of Justin Tomita, Honolulu.*

FIGURE 147. *Withington residence. Living room. (Augie Salbosa, 1981.)*

fortress built of local lava rock set in concrete in the dampness of Manoa Valley, it resonated with Hart Wood's earlier visions of domesticity. Only the house's rear lanai and second-story sleeping porch betrayed its semitropical setting.

In comparison to the abundance of detail and period statement found in the Canavarro, Winslow, and Withington residences, Wood also designed other more modest dwellings in the late 1920s that ostensibly

bear a Colonial mark but take great liberties with the more formal aspects of the style. In many ways reminiscent of the House Electric, examples of this genre include the houses Wood designed for Herbert A. R. Austin (1926) (figs. 149–152), Ernest Van Tassel (1925) (figs. 153–155), and Alexander H. Brodie (1925). These houses are remarkable for their non-symmetrical facades and frequent use of open-beam ceilings and paneled interiors, apparent attempts by Wood to give these somewhat staid New England–inspired residences more a feeling of the warmth of home. In many respects, these quasicolonial houses stand as precursors of some of the nonperiod residential work Wood would design in the 1930s, as these dwellings are more statements in design and craftsmanship than reflections of historic forms. Amalgamated statements alluding to the missionary past of Hawaii, as well as the Islands' more casual tropical ambiance, these houses stand as variations on a theme that Wood would continue to explore during the following decade.

FIGURE 149. *Austin residence, Honolulu.*

FIGURE 150. Opposite. *Austin residence. Main stairway. (Augie Salbosa, 1981.)*

FIGURE 151. *Austin residence. Living room. (Augie Salbosa, 1981.)*

FIGURE 152. *Austin residence. Dining room.*
(Augie Salbosa, 1981.)

FIGURE 153. *Van Tassel residence, Honolulu.*
(David Franzen, 1983.)

FIGURE 154. *Van Tassel residence. Lanai.*
(David Franzen, 1983.)

Several vacation houses—including those designed on Tantalus for Royal Vitousek and the Withington family and the beach houses of Charles R. Frazier and H. D. Sloggett—further perpetuated Wood's sense of the comfortable Hawaiian house. All four employ board and batten walls and have grand, open-beam living rooms. The mountain retreats are both of relatively modest scale and convey a sense of sanctuary and rusticity through their scale and use of materials, including a lava rock fireplace in the Withington cottage. The $15,000 Frazier beach cottage at Lanikai, on the other hand—with its double-pitched hipped roof, large living room, and lanai extending the length of the rear elevation—is an ocean-front summation of the Hawaiian style as it had developed by 1926. In contrast, the more compact beach cottage of H. D. Sloggett in Hanalei (figs. 156 and 157) relied upon the return of Hart Wood's use of a latticed entry, as well as a large, inset, ocean-facing lanai to soften its

FIGURE 155. *Van Tassel residence. Facade. (David Franzen, 1983.)*

RESIDENCE FOR Mʳ H·D· SLOGGETT AT HANALEI, K

HAR·T WOOD   ARCHITECT   HONO

imposing two-story mass and strong peaked gables. In 1931, the architect had another opportunity to work with an oceanfront site when he received the commission to design the Eaton H. Magoon residence at the foot of Diamond Head. This Hawaiian style bungalow with its double-pitched, hipped roofline featured living room walls covered with floor carpeting used in Packard automobiles, painted white—Hart Wood's solution for providing white walls that did not glare.

FIGURE 156. Opposite. *Sloggett Beach House, Hanalei, Kauai. Sketch signed by Wood in 1930. Collection of Justin Tomita, Honolulu.*

FIGURE 157. Above. *Sloggett Beach house. (David Franzen, 1983.)*

THE DEPRESSION
YEARS AND
WORLD WAR II

7

The crash of the stock market in October 1929 did not have an immediate effect upon Hawaii, but by 1931 the depression was being felt in the Islands. By mid-1932, Wood informed his friend Jesse Stanton of Gladding, McBean, "I have managed to keep my office open so far, but I don't know how nor why," and to J. S. Fairweather of Bliss and Fairweather, the successor firm of Bliss and Faville, he confided, "I haven't done enough to pay for expenses for over a year. I thought for a while it was going to miss us, but it was only a little later in coming."[1] The depression struck Wood especially hard, and C. Q. Yee Hop, a local grocery, helped the Wood family get through the roughest trough of the depression, carrying a bill of approximately $1,800 at one point in 1932–1933.

Hart Wood's son, Kenneth Wood, recalled a rare moment of conversation at the usually silent evening meal, when the seriousness of the family's economic situation was discussed. His father asked if anyone had any ideas on how to improve their plight. The young Kenneth suggested that when his father learned that someone was considering erecting a building that perhaps he might go ask if he could design it. From the expression on his father's face it was apparent this suggestion was an approach that had never crossed his mind. Patrons approached an artist, not vice versa.

However, Hart Wood did try the new approach. He made several attempts to be associated with Herbert Cayton Cohen to do the U.S. Immigration Station, writing for support from both former San Francisco architect William A. Newman—who since 1928 had been with the Treasury Department in Washington, D.C.—and Fred M. Kramer of York and Sawyer, who was then in Washington, D.C., supervising the $17.5 million Department of Commerce Building. Unfortunately for Wood, "the office in Washington dictated an association between Cayton and Dickey."[2] Wood also approached Consolidated Amusement for the commission for the Waikiki Theater, another project that eventually landed in the hands of C. W. Dickey.[3] It is intriguing, if fruitless, to contemplate how either of these structures might have emerged if Wood had been involved in their design.

Other than several residential commissions and the Henry Inn Apartments, the only major commission Wood landed in 1931–1932 was the Williams Mortuary on Beretania Street, a two-story masonry building that cost $50,000 (figs. 158–160). The simple but awkwardly handled asymmetrical massing of the building signaled the presence of an insti-

FIGURE 158. *Williams Mortuary, Honolulu. (David Franzen, 1981.) No longer extant.*

FIGURE 159. *Williams Mortuary. Chapel. (David Franzen, 1981.) No longer extant.*

tution straddling the realms of the secular and spiritual. Architectural intimations carrying sacred allusions sprang from the mortuary's design: A vertical element in the form of a flat-roofed, corner tower rose from the front office wing, and a masonry wall demarcated the bounds between the pedestrian ways of the street and the otherworldly realm of the chapel. However, the building was of this world—and more specifically, of Hawaii. Its subdued, solid countenance was enhanced by Chinese columns, coral-paved walkways, a tile, double-pitched hip roof, and masonry screens that perforated the walls. It was not Wood's most inspiring building, but these were not the most inspiring of times.

The depression deepened in 1933. Marking the fifth consecutive year of declining building activity in Hawaii, 1933 saw annual building permit totals for Honolulu drop from $7 million in 1929 to $1.4 million.[4] To help stay economically afloat, Wood relocated his office from downtown to the attic of his Manoa home in March 1933 (fig. 161). From here he would design a number of buildings that further refined his definition of "Hawaiian style" architecture.

The thoughts that Wood and others had articulated throughout the 1920s on appropriate designs for Hawaii crystallized in the summer of 1932 with an exhibition on the topic at the Honolulu Academy of Arts. Invited to give a lecture in conjunction with this exhibition, Wood expanded upon the thoughts he initially enunciated at the opening of Gumps. Wood informed the Academy audience,

FIGURE 160. *Williams Mortuary. (David Franzen, 1981.) No longer extant.*

> When one speaks of a building being Hawaiian then it is a style of
> architecture that expresses friendliness, simplicity and comfort. It is
> the friendliness which most impresses us when we first come here. . . .
> And certainly no building that is lacking in simplicity can "belong" to
> these islands. And after simplicity comes comfort. This is a place of
> comfortable living, and those features of our buildings which make for
> comfort are plenty of window and door openings to admit the cooling
> trade winds, and plenty of shade, expressed by spacious lanais and wide
> overhanging eaves. There are no doubt other characteristic features,
> but these three undoubtedly comprise the chief earmarks of "Hawaiian
> architecture."[5]

Thus to "friendly charm, hospitality, spaciousness and comfort,"[6] Wood now added simplicity.

This framework for defining appropriate Hawaiian design became

FIGURE 161. *Hart Wood's own house in Honolulu. Sketch by Wood. Collection of Justin Tomita, Honolulu.*

evident in houses commissioned by Colin Lennox (1931), J. B. Frietas (1932), Dr. William Mann (1935), and Lanai Plantation for its manager (1936). These residences further developed design concepts initially presented in the diminutive Carey Miller residence of 1926. Although larger in scale than the Miller residence, the massing of these residences effectively conceals their capacious interiors. Also, all four feature board and batten exterior walls. The use of board and batten appears to be a conscious reversion by Wood to an earlier vernacular tradition in Hawaii. Exterior board and batten walls had been in vogue during the late nineteenth century, especially in single-wall buildings.[7] However, by the 1920s the twelve-inch boards with battens had been supplanted by tongue-and-groove lumber in single-wall construction. In double-wall houses, board and batten still figured as a craftsman style interior motif, well revealing the form's associations with rusticity, natural materials, and the products of a nonmachine age; however, it was avoided on the

FIGURE 162. *Freitas residence, Honolulu.*

exterior, with shingles and clapboard being the preferred sheathing. Hart Wood most likely reinstituted this building technique as an exterior wall treatment precisely for the associations that it embodied as an older, simpler form.

The Colin Lennox residence, situated on Makiki Heights, was designed for newlyweds who were former Punahou classmates of Hart Wood Jr. A two-story house, it was sited on its lot so as to allow five mature monkeypod trees to remain intact—and indeed, the house appeared to be nestled in the boughs of these majestic trees. In contrast, the Frietas residence (figs. 162 and 163), located on a terraced lot on

the side of Manoa Valley, had a horizontally flowing design accentuated by a double-pitched "Hawaiian" roof. An inset rear lanai off the corner of the living room provided vistas of Manoa Valley and Diamond Head beyond, as did an out-of-fashion living room bay window. The interior of the living room, with its paneled Douglas fir walls, was brightened by a subdued white finish. This warm yet light effect was produced by painting on a mixture of creosote and gasoline and letting it stand for ten days. Then a coat of plain lime whitewash was applied to the walls. After four days the lime was scrubbed off, and the walls were waxed and rubbed to produce the finished appearance.

Dentist William Mann's residence, perched up on Makiki Heights, also followed a linear flowing floor plan, with a dining room wing digression that opened out to lanais on either side (figs. 164–166). In addition, this handsome two-story house featured Hawaii-inspired decorative elements, including a pair of windows etched with Hawaiian fern motifs. Similarly, the linear progression of the Lanai Plantation manager's house (fig. 167) made for an extremely open and horizontal composition, despite the building's second-floor bedrooms and gabled roofs.

The two-story Herman Ludloff residence (1933) in Hilo (figs. 168–172) differed from its contemporaries, while maintaining a strong sense of regional design. The bold stonework, inset lanai,

FIGURE 164. *Mann residence, Honolulu.*

and double-pitched roof with its large, awkward dormers, a seemingly failed inspiration, all bespeak Hawaii, while the heavy porte cochere, although not integrated into the overall design, appropriately responds to Hilo and its wet weather. In addition, the masterful flared foundation wall appears to emerge from a Japanese tradition and most likely derived from the mason, as it can be found in one or two other houses in Hilo—but nowhere else in the Islands. Again, as in the Frietas residence, Wood resurrects the living room bay window, perhaps a harbinger of charm and comfort for the architect. The living room also included a stage, as the Ludloffs hosted many musical entertainments.

FIGURE 165. *Mann residence.*
Stair rail detail.

FIGURE 166. *Mann residence,*
Honolulu.

FIGURE 167. *Lanai Plantation manager's house, Lanai City.*

FIGURE 168. *Ludloff residence, Hilo, Hawaii. (Augie Salbosa, 1983.)*

FIGURE 169. Opposite. *Ludloff residence. Stone detail. (Augie Salbosa, 1983.)*

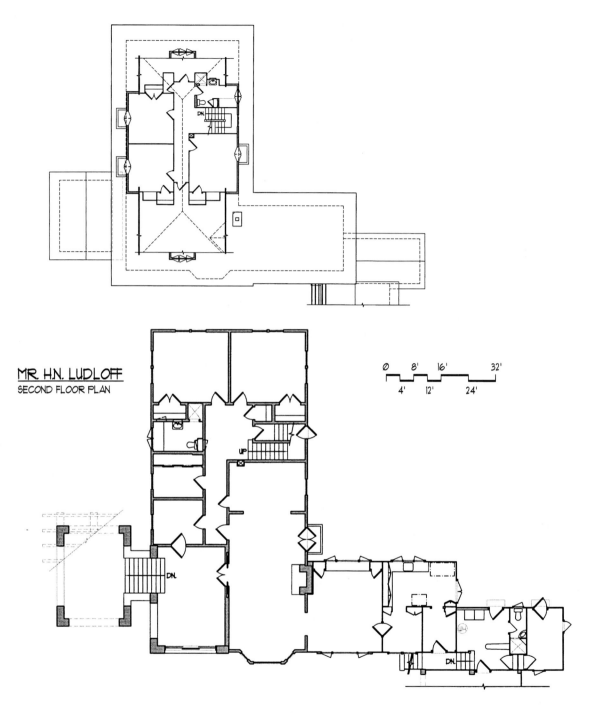

MR. H.N. LUDLOFF
SECOND FLOOR PLAN

Ø 8' 16' 32'

4' 12' 24'

FIGURE 170. *Ludloff residence plan.*

FIGURE 171. Opposite. *Ludloff residence. Porte cochere. (Augie Salbosa, 1983.)*

FIGURE 172. *Ludloff residence.*
Living room. (Augie Salbosa,
1983.)

The simple, friendly, and comfortable Hawaiian design elements incorporated in these residences also emerged in other commissions. The large, 8,000-square-foot, board and batten Waimea Community Center, when opened in 1933, served as the primary public recreation building for this plantation town on the west side of Kauai (figs. 173–175). It housed a basketball court, stage, kitchen, and club rooms and was explicitly erected "for the purpose of character building and development of responsible citizenship."[8]

Embracing such ideals, this exceptionally handsome multipurpose gymnasium presented an imposing yet modestly straightforward statement on civic architecture as an embodiment of the spirit of the Islands. It continued Wood's articulation of a Hawaiian style of architecture with its lofty, prominent roof, large inset lanai, and the incorporation of both local lava rock in the club room fireplace and local sandstone pavers, from nearby Mana, on the low-rising terraces leading to the entry. Masonry columns with embedded lava rock perpetuated the columns earlier introduced in the First Church of Christ Scientist. Large doorways provided ventilation and light to both the gym and club room, giving the building an open, airy feel. The use of local stone in the Community Center was one of the last times such materials would appear in Wood's buildings. The Herman Ludloff residence in Hilo (1933), the Kalihi Uka Pumping Station (1934), and the Lihue United Church (1951) were other late instances in which lava rock was effectively utilized.

Alan Faye, the owner of Waimea Plantation, who had headed the construction committee for the Waimea Community Center, would again call on Wood in 1934 to design a residence for the Waimea Plantation doctor (fig. 176). His brother Lindsay A. Faye, the manager of Kekaha Plantation, would also commission Wood to design several houses for skilled workers. The single-story Waimea Plantation physician's residence

FIGURE 173. *Waimea Community Center, Waimea, Kauai. (Augie Salbosa, 1983.)*

FIGURE 175. Opposite. *Waimea Community Center. Columns at lanai. (Augie Salbosa, 1983.)*

FIGURE 174. *Waimea Community Center.*

broke from the traditional box-shaped house, and through the use of
wings that extended the house in opposite directions at either end, Wood
was able to achieve cross-ventilation for every room. The open, airiness of
the dwelling was further enhanced by a lanai off the rear of the centered
living room.

The six Kekaha Plantation skilled worker houses were similar in

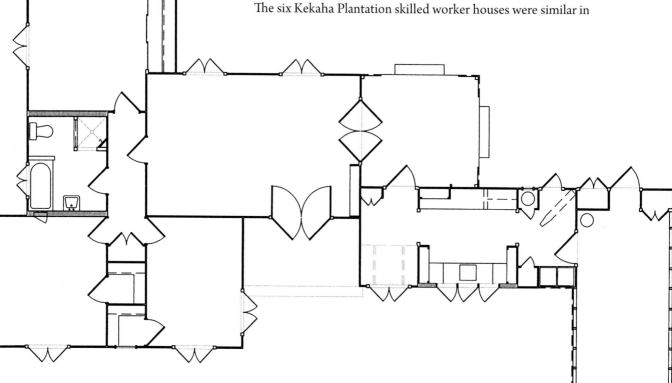

WAIMEA PLANTATION FOR S & E

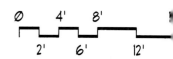

FIGURE 176. *Waimea Plantation*
doctor's house. Floor plan.

design to Waimea's physician's residence. Featuring single-wall construction using twelve-inch tongue and groove, vertical boards, and a shallow pitched hipped roof, these modest homes were attractive yet affordable (fig. 177). As Alan Faye noted, they were "no more expensive than the old-fashioned and less comfortable plantation houses of the past fifty years or more."[9]

The development of these plantation houses followed a tangent pursued by Wood during the period 1920–1939 of architect-designed, moderately priced housing. This continued his earlier interest in designing company towns in California. Shortly after his arrival in Hawaii, he received several commissions for moderately priced houses in recently platted residential tracts. He received several commissions for houses in the Princess Tract during 1920, in which the emphasis was placed on the lanai. For the Diamond Head Terrace tract, he designed four houses in 1924, including one in a Tudor style and another in a style more reminiscent of the missionary houses of the 1830s and 1840s. Another house that called attention to this aspect of Wood's work was built for Dr. Wynn on Pacific Heights, which the newspapers described as "graceful in line although quite simple" and an "example of how attractive a small house can be."[10] During 1935 he also worked on a model FHA house in Waikiki.

In addition to the Waimea and Kekaha Plantation jobs, the sugar industry provided Wood with a major commission in 1934: the $30,000 Administrative Office Building for Ewa Plantation (fig. 178). In an apparent effort to aid the ailing construction industry, Castle & Cooke distributed work to various architects, selecting five architects to each design a building for either its Ewa or Waialua Plantations on Oahu.[11]

In each of the five buildings commissioned by Castle & Cooke, a Hawaiian style roof dominated the design. The sprawling, single-story Ewa Plantation Administration Building, however, was the only one to

feature board and batten walls. The *Honolulu Advertiser* referred to the building as "a model of what might be called Hawaiian architecture" and noted the use of monkeypod panels from Kauai in the main lobby. "Designed for coolness and efficiency,"[12] it utilized both casement and double-hung sash windows for ventilation and was adorned with New England shutters. Sitting on the hot Ewa plain, the building configuration centered on a front patio surrounded by offices, all single stacked to facilitate the flow of the cooling trade winds. The patio originally included a fountain and fishpond framed by potted plants, further enhancing the refreshing atmosphere.

As a result of the Ewa Plantation commission, Wood had the opportunity to work closely with Arthur J. Russell, who served as an advisory architect for Castle & Cooke and oversaw this project. In time the relationship between these two architects grew, and in October 1937 they entered into the partnership of Wood and Russell, which would last until 1941. Russell, a Harvard graduate, had worked for the well-established Boston firms of Peabody and Stearns and Shepley, Rutan and Coolidge, the successor firm to H. H. Richardson. He operated his own office in Boston and then was associated with the firm of Russell and Clinton in New York prior to relocating to Hawaii in 1934. While employed with Castle & Cooke, he oversaw the new building programs for Ewa, Waialua, and Kohala Plantations. Prior to entering into partnership with Wood, he undertook a number of in-house designs for Castle & Cooke, including the nurses' houses, plantation cottages, and clubhouse at Waialua Plantation and also the plantation store in Kohala. In 1940, Castle & Cooke had the new partnership return to Ewa to design

FIGURE 177. *Kekaha skilled worker cottages. (David Franzen, 1981.)*

FIGURE 178. *Ewa Plantation
Administration Building. (Augie
Salbosa, 1981.)*

the E. D. Tenney Center (fig. 179). Dedicated on May 17, 1941, this memorial included an outdoor pool and pool house, which were built as an addition to an existing large auditorium that served a wide variety of community functions. Wood also returned to Kekaha to design that plantation's administrative office in 1938.

Beyond plantation-related commissions, Wood also obtained a contract with the Honolulu Board of Water Supply to design a number of utilitarian structures throughout the city. The semiautonomous Board of Water Supply, under the administration of Frederick Ohrt, had been established in 1930 to replace the mismanaged and scandal-ridden City Waterworks Department, which had brought the city to the verge of a water shortage. Flush with federal funds flowing from the depression-

FIGURE 179. *Tenney Center Pool, Ewa Plantation.*

engendered Public Works Administration, the board assigned four
projects to Wood during the period 1933–1936: the Pacific Heights
Reservoir, the Makiki-Manoa Pumping Station, the Kalihi Uka Pumping
Station, and the Nuuanu Aerator.

Collaborating with landscape architects Robert O. Thompson and
Catherine Richards Thompson, Wood transformed a normally straightforward engineering assignment into a special beauty to behold. By integrating modest, meticulously detailed buildings into a well-manicured,
landscaped setting, this design team produced mini masterpieces of civic
art, three-dimensional declarations that the recently formed Board of
Water Supply was working for the public benefit. By transcending the
normal hope for utilitarian unobtrusiveness, these sensitive and thoughtful designs provided the city with serene green spaces, public amenities
that enhanced their neighborhoods.

In Frederick Ohrt, Hart Wood found a supportive client who
embraced the farsighted vision that utilitarian buildings did not have to
be intrusions inflicted on the community. Ohrt, as the manager and chief
engineer of the Board of Water Supply, worked with Wood over the next
two decades to implement "the policy that beauty need not be sacrificed
to utility and that beauty costs no more than ugliness of neglect, save,
perhaps, a little more thought and planning."[13]

The most straightforward of the four projects was the first: the 1933
Pacific Heights Reservoir and Pumping Station (fig. 180). Situated on
a bend, two-thirds of the way up Pacific Heights Road, Wood fronted
the pump station on the downhill side of its lot. Through asymmetrical,
concrete terraced lawns, the structure flows down the road and up the
hill. A set of steps lends a sense of formality to the site, which is further
enhanced by the pump station's centered, pedimented entry, which is
flanked on either side by concrete grillwork reminiscent of tapa designs.

FIGURE 180. *Pacific Heights Pumping Station, Honolulu. (David Franzen, 1983.)*

The Kalihi Uka Pumping Station (fig. 181), completed in May 1935, faces Kalihi Street, the primary access road for Kalihi Valley. This pumping station deviated from Wood's other Board of Water Supply projects in its use of such prototypical Hawaiian style elements as a tiled, double-pitched hipped roof and lava rock walls. However, its emphasis on a building placed in a landscaped lot remained constant. Sited in the middle of a lawn and elevated on a terrace, the rectangular, thirty-one by

nineteen-foot, Hawaiian style building set forth a distinctive yet unpretentious presence that complemented its residential surroundings. Its studded wooden central doorway, flanked by masonry-screened "windows," further lent an air of domesticity to this handsome composition.

The Makiki Pumping Station (fig. 182), also completed in May 1935, provided water to Makiki Heights and upper Manoa. The semicircular, reinforced concrete pump house, with its centered doorway flanked by masonry grillwork, sits on a terrace fronting on a wading pool, which continues to be utilized by children in the neighborhood. Set at the rear of a large triangular lot, adorned by monkeypod trees and a flowing lawn, the pump station forms a verdant focal point for the fork in the road where Makiki Street splits into Round Top and Makiki Heights Drives.

The fourth WPA project, the Nuuanu Aerator (fig. 183) provided Honolulu with yet another handsome wayside. Located on the original Pali Road (now Old Pali Road) and completed in September 1936, its purpose was to purify surface waters drawn from Nuuanu Stream. The plastered concrete block structure was unobtrusively nestled in a cluster of kukui nut trees and was dematerialized by perforating masonry screens. At night the aerator was lit, allowing passersby to observe the percolating water being aerated. An expansive, rolling lawn again effectively set off the building, and a stone-lined *auwai* (ditch), terminating at a lily pond, placed a water element before the public view and defined the space. The aerator augmented the gardenlike appearance of Honolulu and reminded the public that such an appearance was made possible thanks to the availability of water.

FIGURE 181. Opposite. *Kalihi Uka Pumping Station, Honolulu. (David Franzen, 1983.)*

FIGURE 183. *Nuuanu Aerator facility.*

FIGURE 182. Opposite. *Makiki Pumping Station. (David Franzen, 1983.)*

Through these Board of Water Supply projects, Wood further developed his thoughts with regard to the symbiotic relationship between a building and its environmental setting. Neither dominated the other, but rather each was an integral part of the whole. These projects also signaled Wood's first forays into what might be considered modern design. By 1937, the sleek, unadorned flat-roofed forms of the modern style had asserted themselves into Hawaii's design vocabulary. In recognition of this shift, the Honolulu Academy of Arts in August of that year set forth an exhibition to further promote the community's understanding of the subject. The display featured Wood's Makiki-Manoa Pumping Station, as well as C. W. Dickey's Waikiki Theater and residential projects by Ray Morris, Vladimir Ossipoff, Claude Albon Stiehl, and Albert Ely Ives.[14] The last three architects and the firm of Dahl and Conrad were closely associated with the new modern movement, and in the ensuing years, prior to the advent of World War II, they would garner the majority of the custom-designed residential and apartment commissions.

The ascendancy of a new, modern, tropical style of architecture was reiterated in the February 12, 1938, *Honolulu Star-Bulletin*'s special section, "Grow with Honolulu, Invest in a Home." Residential commissions of Claude Stiehl and Alvin Shadinger and C. W. Dickey's Wilcox Memorial Hospital illustrated this twelve-page insert, and articles written by Connie Conrad, Ray Morris, C. W. Dickey, and Hart Wood discussed the current scene. C. W. Dickey noted,

> We are living in an age of wonderful progress in architecture and building. The changes are about us on every side, and even those indifferent to architecture can not fail to notice it. There is a freshness of spirit about the new work that sets it apart from the old.
>
> After years of slavish copying of old world architectural forms, the

architects of today are showing real originality and imagination, and are creating new forms, and there is an entirely new feeling and atmosphere in their work.[15]

Dickey went on to credit such new building materials as stainless steel, chromium plating, asbestos, aluminum, molded and structural glass, air conditioning, and especially moderately priced hollow cement blocks for helping to make possible the new trends in architecture. In other articles, Morris and Conrad further described the new flat-roofed houses with their "elusive quality of clean cut lines and large plain surfaces," usually painted white, and the "free flow of line and mass, instilling restfulness and freedom which is essential to a semi tropical condition."[16] In his article, Ray Morris acknowledged that the flat roof's "straight severe line" was "more suited to modern design"; however, he still maintained that the Hawaiian style roof was "the best suited roof for this community."

In the midst of these pronouncements on progress, Hart Wood offered words of caution:

Recently someone bemoaned Honolulu's loss of charm. Those of us who have been here longer realize that the plaint was not without some merit.

That Honolulu has lost some of its charm is undeniable. That for this there are some compensations is no doubt also a fact.

. . . It seems natural to deplore the vanishing of the "good old days" and to forget the present good.

Honolulu during the decade ending 1930 was one of the fastest growing cities under the U.S. flag. . . . With such growth come the disadvantages as well as the advantages of progress.

One does not have to go back very far to recall the time when the best buildings of the islands were almost completely lacking in architectural pretensions and deficient if not devoid of modern conveniences—houses not weather tight, insufficient light, and inconveniently and uneconomically planned.

City streets and country roads largely in the horse and buggy days, water supply inadequate, infrequent deliveries, boat service slower, and less comfortable; and in many other ways the comforts and conveniences which we now take for granted were absent. . . .

And yet that nostalgic call which most of us feel is for a certain something that is not without substance.

In fact it is of the utmost value, for it represents the essence of life in the islands; that which embodies the charm, friendliness, simplicity and comfort of Hawaii: which is the lure that calls and recalls countless thousands to its shores; that causes unnumbered hosts to sing its praises and that binds us, its favored inhabitants, with invisible and insoluble bands to this Aloha Land.

Such things may be elusive, they may be intangible, but they can be expressed in buildings.

They should be expressed in some measure in all island buildings and it is one of the architect's civic obligations to the community to see that they are.

In the glitter and glamour of movie land architecture we are apt to forget the weightier things of real life.

It is up to the architects of the islands to steer a straight course, to keep our heads, to keep abreast of progress, but not to forget the rich heritage of the past.

In other words, to consciously strive to retain in our work the charm, friendliness and simplicity that is Hawaii.[17]

Wood's article may have simplified the architectural achievements
of the past and misread the motivations of the modern movement. However, his reminder of the need to remain steadfast in the architectural
embodiment of the Spirit of Aloha would continue to resound down the
corridor of time. It would be a recurring point of orientation for Hawaii's
architectural community as it found itself caught in the midst of the der-
vish rush toward a Bauhaus-inspired celebration of the machine and the
economic-scientific perspective of the world.

Wood ended the decade of the 1930s with a three-month trip with
his family to the continental United States, not returning to Hawaii until
December 13, 1939 (fig. 184). Traveling across country from Los Angeles to Washington, D.C., by train, the Woods attended the annual AIA
meeting in the nation's capital, where Hart Wood was one of Hawaii's
two delegates. Following the meeting, the family visited New York City,
Boston, and Philadelphia before heading west in a newly purchased
Ford to San Francisco. The journey back to California retraced Hart
Wood's initial migration across country, with stops in Wichita and Hays,
Kansas, Denver, and ultimately San Francisco. Places of his youth were
revisited and old friends and family looked up. During the ten days
the architect stayed in New York City, he visited the 1939 World's Fair
several times. His personal log of the trip showed much of the first day
at the fair was spent at the Town of Tomorrow, with its nineteen or so
different houses. Most of the houses displayed period revival forms,
although there were also three or four in a modern vein. He found only
three or four of the houses to be any good, one of which was modern,
but the remainder received judgments ranging from "so-so" to "ordinary." Details caught his eye: "Bath room with mirrored walls," "Pool
extending into lanai," "draped walls in Bed Rooms," and "sliding glass
doors." He returned three more times to take in the "City of Tomorrow"

show in the Perisphere, General Motors' "Streets of Tomorrow" display, the stroboscopic lights at General Electric and Westinghouse's pavilions, and a myriad of other exhibits that probed a technology-filled utopian future.[18]

FIGURE 184. *Hart and Jessie Wood, ca. 1939.*

That Wood was interested in modern architecture is obvious from his recorded statements and the evolution of his architectural design, as expressed in several projects done just before the onset of World War II. In an article entitled "Hawaii People Appreciate Good Architecture," Wood further articulated his views on the changing architectural scene: "Modern architecture in a general way consists of cubical or rectangular masses, sometimes curiously assembled and even more curiously supported; of large expanses of wall surface, usually white, and large expanses of glass. As a rule there is little or no ornament."[19]

The article went on to quote Hart Wood as saying, "modern design brought the first breath of vitality to architecture that it has had in many a century." However, most of the buildings he cited as examples of great American architecture were classicist or revival styles, such as Trinity Church in Boston, Madison Square Garden, and the Washington Capitol.

Wood did not view modern architecture with the same eyes as the movement's major proponents, such as Sigfried Giedion, who exhorted, "There is a word we should refrain from using to describe contemporary architecture. This is the word 'style.' The moment we fence architecture within a notion of 'style,' we open the door to a formalist approach. The contemporary movement is not a 'style' . . . it is an approach to life that slumbers unconsciously within us all."

Hart Wood appears to have treated Modernism in the same manner as other styles: as another tool in his design quiver. He recognized the growing popularity of the forms and their economic advantages and utilized them. As a rule, however, the buildings he designed in the later years of his career almost always retained at least some vestiges of that modern no-no—ornamentation—whether Classical or those with more local references.

The most significant projects Wood and Russell completed

immediately before the war included the Board of Water Supply's Engineering Offices and the Pearl Harbor Branch of the Bank of Hawaii, both of which reflected the modern genre. The Engineering Offices (figs. 185 and 186) came into Wood and Russell's office in 1939. This rather straightforward, reinforced concrete structure followed a U-shaped plan, with its two wings cascading down Lisbon and Alapai Streets, dropping from three to two stories on the Lisbon side and from one and a half to one story on the other. A band of glass block windows, integrated with steel sash windows that have been recently replaced, wraps around the building's public faces, contributing to its flow in a very modern manner. The windows provide the only relief to the building's flat plastered walls, other than the entry at the right corner of the facade. The entry is sheltered by a flat-roofed, cantilevered marquee that wraps around the right corner, further advancing the modern mode. Inscribed on the front of the marquee are the words "Pure Water is Man's Greatest Need—Conserve It," and on the Lisbon Street side is found the Hawaiian saying, *Uwe ka lani ola ka honua*, which means, "When the heavens weep the earth lives." The Hawaiian cultural presence is amplified in a pair of bas-reliefs, sculpted from green Vermont slate by Honolulu artist Margarite Blasingame, which flank the entry doors. These dramatically depict the Hawaiian legend of Kane and Kanaloa's bringing water to the Islands. The lobby further conveys the water theme with its green tile floors and green walls, while sleek chrome-plated bronze railings continue the modern message. An early Juliette May Fraser mural depicting the uses of water on the island of Oahu also graces the lobby. The courtyard area enclosed by the wings functioned as the agency's base yard, the site's former use.

The drawings for the Bank of Hawaii branch at Pearl Harbor were completed on the first of May 1941 by Hart Wood and Arthur Russell Architects. Their office was still the Wood home. The bank building

FIGURE 185. *Board of Water Supply Engineering Building, Honolulu.*

was the most modernistic structure done by Wood up to that point in his career. The bank is a simple two-story rectangle with a hipped roof covered with green flat clay tile and with smooth stucco walls (fig. 187). Its large, multilight stainless steel window frames are decorated with stainless steel stars, one for each light of glass around the perimeter. The flat canopy over the front entrance had a decorative stainless steel fascia, and planters surrounded three sides of the building. Although somewhat austere on the exterior, this modest modern bank's interior included a

FIGURE 186. *Board of Water
Supply Engineering Building,
Honolulu.*

FIGURE 187. Opposite. *Bank of
Hawaii, Pearl Harbor Branch.*

second-floor mezzanine with a stainless steel railing decorated with ship silhouettes, and air-conditioning grillwork ornamented with abstracted leaf patterns.

The War Years

Like most architects in Hawaii, Wood closed his office shortly after the onset of World War II, and it remained closed most or all of 1942. At the end of the year he was commissioned to handle the design for the Passenger and Freight Terminal at Honolulu Airport, which called for buildings and other improvements with a cost of up to $12 million. He was alone in the office at the time and spent much of 1943 working on this project, which would never be implemented, as his work was stopped by other military developments after he had only finished the preliminary design. Following the termination of the airport project, Wood went to work for the territorial government in 1944, joining the staff of the Post War Planning Division for about one year.[20] The fruits of this stint appeared in a September 1944 *Paradise of the Pacific* article, proposing a new, never realized civic center to be built in Kakaako. Wood also busied himself with the local chapter of the American Institute of Architects (AIA), being elected president for the third time in 1943. He had cofounded Hawaii's AIA chapter in 1925 and served as its second president in 1926.

During this period of global conflict, Wood also was struck by personal tragedy when his son, Lt. Thomas Wood, was killed in western Europe on August 17, 1944. The loss of Thomas profoundly affected Hart Wood's wife, Jessie, causing a breakdown from which she never fully recovered.[21]

REOPENING
HIS OFFICE

8

Following the war, Wood was almost immediately busy upon reopening his office. Original drawings, dated June 19, 1944, exist for a small residence for J. Walsh on Terrace Drive in Manoa. In addition, during the first month of 1946, plans for two residential renovations were ready for bidding, and the Bertram Quinn residence was under construction on a small, low-lying flag lot in Nuuanu Dowsett. Considered a "problem" lot, Wood "made an asset of every deficit," and the property "became the setting for a home that well illustrates Hawaii's way of life."[1] The two-story board and batten dwelling placed the garage within the body of the house, on the ground floor adjoining the kitchen and living room. A fireplace was a focal point in the living room, a feature that Hart Wood felt was "becoming a 'must' in island homes." Off the living room was an outdoor, glass-roofed lanai, which could serve as a dining area. The second floor included a large inset lanai that was accessed from each of the two bedrooms.

Within a year, Wood's problem did not involve utilization of a flag lot but rather how to get everything done. He continued to do residential jobs, but the bulk of his work now was for the Territory of Hawaii and the Board of Water Supply. Prior to the war, in early 1940, Wood had taken the lead in arguing for good design for public projects and for the privatization of public design work. Much of the public building design of the time was done in-house by the Territorial Department of Public Works, which was headed by Louis Cain.

In February and early March of 1940, a group of local architects, headed by Hart Wood, who was a member of the Planning Board, objected to the design of an addition to the Judiciary Building (Aliiolani Hale). In a February 24, 1940, letter to the editor of *The Honolulu Advertiser*, he set forth detailed arguments about what was wrong with the design of the addition.[2] While advocating for awarding more public works design projects to private, local architects, he also pointed out the mistakes made with the design of the Territorial Office Building, Aloha Tower, and city incinerator. Someone must have been listening to his words, for after World War II the Territory of Hawaii would be one of Wood's major patrons. Within the five-year period from 1946 to 1951, he received contracts for the Paauilo Elementary and Intermediate School, Molokai Elementary School, the Liliuokalani Building, and Waimano Home Hospital, as well as the Honolulu Board of Water Supply's Administration Building and a number of pumping stations. With so many major commissions coming to his office, Wood had to expand.

By October 1946 he had added a part-time helper and had offered a position to Roger Benezet, who joined him later that year.[3] William Burgett was offered a position in the firm on December 18, 1946, and left Los Angeles for Hawaii on January 25, 1947.[4] Prior to departing, he obtained plans or measured California water supply buildings for Wood's reference in designing the new administrative building for the Honolulu Board of Water Supply.[5] By June 1947, six people were working in Wood's office, and he was actively seeking two more drafters, especially those with structural engineering experience.[6] Wood was sufficiently comfort-

able with the capabilities of both Benezet and Burgett that, near the end
of 1947, he went on an eight-to-ten-week trip to the mainland (fig. 188).
He advised Lyman Bigelow, the superintendent of buildings, that in his
absence, his "associates," Roger P. Benezet and William S. Burgett, would
be in charge of his office and business.[7]

The following year, Wood entered into partnership with Edwin A.
Weed. Weed had been a practicing architect since 1934 and was registered in several eastern states. In 1935 he was registered as a structural
and mechanical engineer. According to a resume that Wood put together
for the army on May 5, 1949, Weed was "experienced principally in engineering construction methods, specification writing, supervision and job
management."[8] It is likely that this continued to be his primary role in his
partnership with Wood, at least for the first few years.

The enormously busy, twilight years of Wood's career would be
characterized by attempts to strike a balance between keeping "abreast
of progress" and recalling the rich heritage of Hawaii. This period not
only signaled a shift in the character of Wood's commissions but also in
his design motifs. Markedly modern in appearance, a new austerity was
introduced into Wood's work of the late 1940s. The amount of ornamentation was reduced and handled in a less obvious manner. Following the
formation of his partnership with Edwin A. Weed, Wood's hand becomes
less clearly recognized in many of his later commissions. However, the
attention to detail, engaging color palates, and variation of textures and
surfaces should be attributed to him.

The office completed work on Paauilo Elementary and Intermediate School on August 15, 1947, with Roger Benezet checking the drawings. This is a very simple, primarily wood building in a modernist style:
very horizontal, thanks to horizontal wood siding, long rows of awning
windows, and a fairly flat roof with a clerestory. Except for the use of lava

FIGURE 188. *Hart Wood, ca. 1947.*

rock fieldstone at the entry and a design that maximized natural ventilation, very little ties this building to Wood's Hawaiian Regionalist past. This is similarly true for the other school projects he did at the time, including the Molokai Elementary School.

Douglas Yanagihara, who was hired by Wood as a drafter in 1947, remembered that both the Wyllie Street and Wailupe Pumping Stations were completed for the Board of Water Supply shortly before he arrived in the office. The Wyllie Street Pumping Station is centered at the end of its namesake street, and its symmetrical facade, which climbs the hillside it abuts, is the focal point of the street. Unlike many of the other pumping stations designed by Wood, this has virtually no grounds in front of it and practically no ornamentation. However, the backdrop was planted in *hau,* and the strong forms and simple decorative gate give the pumping station a fairly strong presence on the street.

The Wailupe Pumping Station is not nearly as successful. It is a simple block of a building with a ridiculously small, Classically styled fountain pasted to its front and no site design worth mentioning. It seems hard to believe that Wood himself paid much attention to this building during its design. It is more likely that his attention was focused on three other significant commissions that began in 1947. In that year, work began in earnest on the Board of Water Supply Administration Building, the Liliuokalani Building, and the Waimano Home Hospital. As a result of these projects, in February 1948 Hart Wood had to inform Lt. Col. G. M. Cookson at Fort Ruger that he could not help with work at Fort DeRussey, especially any projects that were in a hurry.

The first of the three large projects to be completed was the Waimano Home Hospital Building (fig. 189). Done for the Territorial Department of Institutions, the main building housed the administration offices and had two wings for mentally disabled girls. Sited at the top of the

FIGURE 189. *Waimano Home Hospital Building.*

Waimano Home grounds on Maunalani Heights, the building presided over the complex and offered splendid views of the Pearl Harbor area. This highly asymmetric plan is one of the most modernist of the projects to come from Wood's office. The bands of windows, roof overhangs, and rough block patterns all emphasized the horizontality of the building. The building is primarily two stories, with a partial third lower floor at the eastern side of the building. Most of the attention to detail was spent on the entry lobby. The exterior "Hollo-Ston" finish is wrapped into the lobby, which is meticulously detailed through the use of koa paneling and the different grid pattern employed for the fenestration of the space.

The $400,000 building was completed in 1949. Also completed about the same time were service buildings for the Waimano Home complex, valued at $275,000.

The Liliuokalani Building (figs. 190 and 191) was the next completed, with bids opened for this territorial office building on November 5, 1948. This large $1 million building is in most respects a simple modernist building. Constructed of plastered concrete and concrete

FIGURE 190. *Liliuokalani Building, Honolulu.*

FIGURE 191. *Liliuokalani Building. Main entry. (Robert Wenkam, ca. 1950.)*

masonry, it is four stories tall with a partially exposed basement level. The building is arranged in an L shape, with the two legs set back from but oriented to the streets that once ran past the building. Most likely, the configuration was in part a result of the shape of the lot, but it also served to break up what would otherwise be an uncomfortably long facade. The windows are steel, arranged in continuous strips, with the first story windows going from floor nearly to the ceiling and the upper stories somewhat narrower. The lobby is relatively plain, with some decorative metal trims around the elevators and koa trims in parts of the interior.

One of the most interesting characteristics of the building is the decorative treatment of the entry. This focal point is framed with a bold, square arch of Carrera marble, at the center of which is a sculpture of male and female Hawaiians, clad in the apparel of Hawaiian royalty, such as feather cloaks and a feathered helmet for the male figure. This sculpture at the apex of the square arch seems at odds with the Modernism of the building. The entry was further emphasized by planters and paving of granite and two Moderne flagpoles, one on each side of the entry in planters. The Liliuokalani Building opened on June 28, 1950.

By December of 1948, Wood's office was working overtime to meet the January 31, 1949, deadline for the Board of Water Supply Administration Building.[9] The firm also continued work on several other Board of Water Supply projects. The St. Louis Heights Pumping Station was designed at about this time,[10] and the Palolo Valley Pumping Station for the Board of Water Supply was completed in 1950. An addition to the Board of Water Supply Engineering Building was also in the planning stages in May 1949.

The Board of Water Supply Administration Building (figs. 192–194) is certainly the crowning achievement of Wood's last years of practice. It is an interesting building for both its design and the questions it raises about how much Wood actually had to do with the design, particularly since it wasn't completed until five years after Wood ceased active practice.[11] In fact, it was not dedicated until after he had passed away. It is known that during construction, some details were changed. For example, at the exterior wall near the main entry, a change was made from green plaster to green marble after he was no longer at the firm, and refinements to the canopy columns were also made after he was no longer active with the firm. However, the design of the building was completed by early 1949, and the changes made were minor compared to the overall design.

FIGURE 192. *Board of Water Supply Administration Building, Honolulu.*

FIGURE 193. Opposite. *Board of Water Supply Administration Building, Honolulu.*

UWE KA LANI OLA KA HONUA

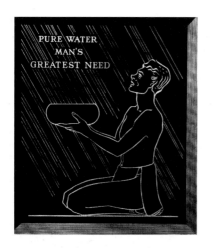

FIGURE 194. *Board of Water Supply Administration Building, Honolulu.*

In plan the building is a relatively simple, rectangular, three-story structure, but in every other respect it reflects Wood's version of Modernism. Its horizontal line and use of the modernist brise-soleils is modified by the Chinese-inspired design of the brise-soleils on the Beretania Street facade of the building. In addition, the Japanese flavor of the entry canopy is a distinctly Wood touch to its most public facade. The building's subtle Asian articulations further flow forth in the ultramodern, curved pedestrian bridge, with its two support pylons, which connects the main offices with the earlier Engineering Building.

These exterior details were all part of an orchestrated effort by Wood to unify architecture, landscape, and art to convey a message not only about the Board of Water Supply but about water and the community as a whole. In back of the symbolic water fountain are the Hawaiian words *Uwe ka lani ola ka honua*, which earlier appeared in the Engineering Building marquee. In the lobby is a large mural by Juliette May Fraser that illustrates the importance of water in Hawaiian cosmology as well as for practical purposes. The combination of Western, Asian, and Hawaiian themes is typical of much of Wood's best work in Hawaii. The generous landscaped yard fronting the building—and inside, the inclusion of a strategically placed fish tank, a ubiquitous use of green, and koa wood paneling and cabinetry in the lobby—reinforce the design intent.

Wood's involvement with the Board of Water Supply and the patron-like manner with which he was treated by Fred Ohrt, longtime head of the Board of Water Supply, would have assured that this important building had Wood's fullest attention. It is symbolic of their dedication to each other that Orht retired the same year that Wood stopped practicing architecture.

In May 1949, Wood's office included Edwin Weed and four drafters.[12] This was a large staff for Wood and reflected the torrid pace of his

FIGURE 195. *Lihue United Church, Lihue, Kauai. (David Franzen, 1983.)*

work in the previous two years. By late 1949, his staff had been reduced by two drafters,[13] in part the result of the very lengthy dock strike of 1949, which strangled Hawaii's economy.[14]

In 1950 Hart Wood was seventy years old and—at least in terms of volume of work—probably more successful than at any time in his career practicing alone. His confidence in the future of the office was sufficient that he began looking for office space outside his Manoa Street home.[15] At this time, he was given the green light to design the Lihue United Church (fig. 195), a project that Wood had been discussing with Elsie Wilcox and Digby Sloggett since at least 1933.

Completed in 1951, the church is in most respects a throwback to the First Church of Christ Scientist. It uses moss rock walls, a steep, rather thin wood-deck gable roof supported on large rafters, cast concrete window and door frames, and a stone steeple with cast concrete elements that have a slight, modern Gothic flair. The newest building was clearly designed to be resonant of its neighboring Parish Hall of 1921.[16]

Also in 1950, Wood designed a residence for his eldest son, Hart Wood Jr.[17]

In 1951 the office prepared the design for Molokai Elementary School. The drawings are dated March 3, 1951, and signed by both Edwin Weed and Hart Wood, each listed as architect. Hart Wood's signature looks shaky and presages the end of his career. Notes on drawings indicate drawn by "JL" (John Lau) and checked by "EW" (Edwin Weed). The relatively undistinguished design consisted of two concrete block buildings connected by a covered walkway. The open-air lobby had a "trellis" (really a grille) at the front entry as a decorative element.

THE CREPUSCULAR
YEARS, THE END
OF A CAREER

9

Following the completion of the Lihue United Church, age began to catch up to Hart Wood. By June 1952, when he was admitted to Maunalani Hospital, he "couldn't hold a pencil," nor could he take care of himself. Probably suffering from Parkinson's disease, this talented architect would live out his days at Maunalani Hospital.[1] His house was sold, and it was about this time that Wood's firm moved to the Hawaiian Life Building.

Although Wood stayed at Maunalani Hospital, it is likely that he continued some form of control over the design of projects in the office for a time. There is a set of drawings for a U.S. Navy mine storage building dated October 3, 1952, and initialed as checked by Hart Wood.[2] Although Weed led the firm for several years after Wood retired, various documents and interviews show him to be dependent on others for design.[3] According to his daughter-in-law, Patty Wood, the Board of Water Supply Kuliouou Booster Station (fig. 196) was the last job with which Hart Wood had a lot of involvement. Located at the corner of Elelupe Street and Kalanianaole Highway, it was completed in May 1956, but the date on the front proclaims 1954. Although hospitalized at Maunalani, Wood was able to visit this site during construction thanks to his family taking him on car rides.

243

FIGURE 196. *Kuliouou Booster Station, Honolulu.*

As with most of his Board of Water Supply buildings, the property is well landscaped, again the work of landscape architects Bob and Catherine Thompson. The building is set back fifty feet from the highway, with a planter raised above the natural terrain by about eighteen inches. The pumping station itself is a relatively simple, modern design. It relies on the use of grids for its surface articulation. The two forms of the building overlap, with the lower foremost block having a light grid pattern and supporting the sign of the station. The taller building volume set slightly farther back is framed with a raised edge, and the grid is very bold, emphasized by color and in relief. In many ways it reflects Wood's 1938 description of modern architecture, with its large expanses of wall surface and its cubical or rectangular masses, which might be considered "curiously assembled."

This concluded Hart Wood's career as an architect. The words of Hope Dennis, who interviewed Wood for a newspaper article in 1954, still ring true, if in hindsight understated. Her story's concluding line noted, "This beloved grand old man of architecture can look back on a professional career spent in contributing to Hawaii's fine architecture."[4]

Conclusion

The death of Hart Wood on October 6, 1957, put an exclamation point on the first and arguably the greatest era of Hawaiian Regionalism. The 1950s would see the emergence of other greats in Hawaii's architectural design community who eschewed overt ornamentation completely, but who still used spatial relationships, rooflines, lanais, materials, and ventilation and who showed sensitivity to the importance of landscape design in ways that Hart Wood probably would have appreciated. None of these young masters, except perhaps Vladimir Ossipoff, would prove to be as capable as Wood in so comfortably synthesizing Asian and Western forms.

The limited attempts at regionalism in the opening decades of the twentieth century, prior to Hart Wood's arrival in Hawaii, largely involved using transplanted forms from the Mediterranean or Mission Revival styles, a practice that many architects continued through the 1930s. He pioneered a design language that was unique to Hawaii and did so by looking not only at its benign weather but by using local materials in innovative ways and incorporating the cultures of the various people of Hawaii. The latter alone is sufficient to elevate Wood above his contemporaries. In addition, he took the lanai, a popular residential form since the late 1870s, and expanded its use into the realm of ecclesiastical architecture and explored its suitability in public buildings such as the Waimea Community Center.

Although Dickey, a powerful design talent himself, far outstripped Wood in the sheer number of commissions his office produced and ultimately had more influence on Hawaii's architectural community, Wood's unique artistic vision remains unmatched, and his best works will always be icons of Hawaiian architecture.

NOTES

Chapter 1: *Influences of Youth*

1. Hart Wood was also the great-grandson of James and Catherine Wood. James Wood (b. 1774/1775), an emigrant from Ireland, married into a German Lutheran family settled in York County, Pennsylvania. A farmer, James came to own significantly valued real estate by the mid-nineteenth century. The Wood family was large, with eight known sons and two daughters born between about 1800 and 1830 in Pennsylvania and Virginia. The children of James and Catherine Wood were John (b. 1801/1802), two other sons born between 1800 and 1810, Elizabeth (b. 1812/1813), Alexander (b. 1813/1814), William (b. 1814/1815), a daughter born between 1815 and 1820, Samuel (b. 1817), and two sons born between 1825 and 1830. (The dates of birth are approximate, derived from the ages of individuals listed in the census and taking into account the date of documentation.) Most of the male children became farmers. Two, however—William and Samuel—became carpenters. (See also n. 10.) "James Wood, Brownsville, Fayette County," *Pennsylvania Census*, 1830, 221; *Pennsylvania Census*, 1850, 314; "Joseph Wood, Brownsville Township, Fayette County," *Pennsylvania Census*, 1870, 2; and, "Elizabeth Wood, Luzerne Township, Fayette County," *Pennsylvania Census*, 1870, 243. Also see the indices for the *Pennsylvania and Virginia Census*, 1800–1870.

2. Samuel Wood married Lucy Curl, daughter of James Curl. The James Curl family was also largely agrarian. James (b. 1876/1877) married into the John Hart family, German Lutherans with ties in both Pennsylvania and Virginia. (See also n. 10.) Lucy, like her husband, was born in Virginia (1818/1819). Known children of Samuel and Lucy Wood were Gibson (b. 1840/1841), Mary (b. 1842/1843), Thomas (b. 1844), Louis (b. 1846), Charles (b. 1848/1849), and Lucy (b. 1852/1853). "Samuel Wood, Bridgeport Borough, Fayette County," *Pennsylvania Census*, 1850, 330; and *Pennsylvania Census*, 1870, 257.

3. *Kansas*, volume in *The United States Biographical Dictionary* (Chicago and Kansas City: S. Lewis & Company, 1879), 452–453. Louis Wood may have lived with his mother's family, the Curls, while attending Waynesburg College. By about 1840, the James Curl family had settled in Cumberland, Greene County. Waynesburg College was

located in the immediate vicinity. Following Waynesburg, Louis "took a two years special course in the study of architecture and kindred arts at Cornell University." William G. Cutler, *History of the State of Kansas* (Chicago: Alfred T. Andreas, 1883), 583; John M. Peterson, *John G. Haskell: Pioneer Kansas Architect* (Lawrence: Douglas County Historical Society, 1984), 81–82; "James Curl, Cumberland, Greene County," *Pennsylvania Census*, 1840, 106; and "Hiram, John, Remembrance, and Thomas Curl," four Curl family listings, *Pennsylvania Census*, 1850, 114, 111, 117, and 100. Louis M. H. Wood's university training in architecture was among the earliest of its kind in the United States. The Massachusetts Institute of Technology (MIT) had initiated formal study in 1868, with a two-year program in architecture. Cornell opened the second American program in 1871, but its formal courses were set up in a four-year framework (another first of its type). Both universities had only one professor of architecture for the course of study. Charles Babcock, trained in the office of Richard Upjohn in the 1850s, *was* Cornell's architectural program during the first half of the 1870s. Morris Bishop, *A History of Cornell* (Ithaca, New York: Cornell University Press, 1962), 160–161, 169.

4. "T. H. B. Wood, Hays, Ellis County," *Kansas Agricultural Census*, 1885, 16. Children of T. H. B. and Maggie Wood were listed as Hart (b. 1880), Harry (b. 1882/1883), and Ada (b. 1883/1884). Also, letters from Mary Ann Thompson, Kansas Room Librarian, Hays Public Library, to Karen J. Weitze, November 10, 1986, and December 2, 1986. Ms. Thompson summarized T. H. B. Wood's chronology of building trades employment in Hays, citing material appearing in the local newspapers and archival records.

5. *Kansas*, 1879, 452–453; and Peterson, *John G. Haskell*, 1984, 81–82.

6. Peterson, *John G. Haskell*, 1984, 1–6; Frank W. Blackmar (ed.), *Kansas: A Cyclopedia of State History, Embracing Events, Institutions, Industries, Counties, Cities, Towns, Prominent Persons, Etc.* (Chicago: Standard Publishing Company, 1912); E. F. Caldwell, *A Souvenir History of Lawrence, Kansas* (Kansas City, Missouri: Lawton and Burnap, 1898); Richard Cordley (Plymouth Congregational Church), *A History of Lawrence, Kansas, from the Earliest Settlement to the Close of the Rebellion* (Lawrence, Kansas: E. F. Caldwell/ Lawrence Journal Press, 1895). John Gideon Haskell (1832–1907) was the eldest son of a New England family. He apprenticed as a carpenter in Wilbraham, Massachusetts (near Springfield), at seventeen and took a year of courses in engineering and mathematics at Brown University in Providence, Rhode Island, at twenty-two. Haskell then worked as a draftsman in Boston, following his family to Lawrence, Kansas, in 1857. The Haskells had gone to Lawrence as members of the second group sent there by the abolitionist New Emigrant Aid Company in 1854. John's father Franklin established the Congregational Church in Lawrence—the town's first church—and served as its deacon. Dudley Chase Haskell (1842–1883), the fourth and last Haskell child, arrived in Lawrence the next year (1855). In Kansas, John G. Haskell built a substantial business. The Haskells' 160-acre farmstead in Lawrence was a focus of life in the developing community, as was the later Haskell Institute.

7. Peterson, *John G. Haskell*, 1984, 67–167.

8. See n. 4. The 1885 *Kansas Agricultural Census* lists both Harry and Ada as born in Kansas. The Thomas H. B. Wood family must have made the move in 1882 or 1883, before the arrival of Harry.

9. The Thomas H. B. Wood family arrived in Hays in about mid-1884. (See n. 13.) The family may have spent a full year or two in Lawrence, extending their stay through the births of Harry (1882/1883) and Ada (1883/1884).

10. Letters from Thompson to Weitze, November 10, 1986, and December 2, 1986. As Lutheran pastor in Hays, Thomas H. B. Wood was a latter-day extension of multigenerational, multifamily Pennsylvania German traditions. The John Hart, James Wood, and James Curl families were intricately intertwined from the late-eighteenth through the mid-nineteenth centuries. (See nn. 1 and 2.) Each family concentrated its households in the counties of York and Westmoreland initially and then by 1830 settled in the far western counties of Fayette and Greene. A pattern of movement between these German Lutheran Pennsylvania counties and the Shenandoah Valley in Virginia existed for the three families. Movement was from Pennsylvania to Virginia, through the Cumberland Gap, with thirty-one Lutheran and Reformed congregations established in nine Virginia and West Virginia counties by 1776. Pennsylvania pastors had the primary responsibility for serving the Virginia congregations. For the Hart, Wood, and Curl families, migration focused in ca. 1800, ca. 1816, and ca. 1840. Judging from the family birth rates recorded in the Pennsylvania and Virginia census records, each stay was short—about half a dozen years. In the case of the John Hart family, the wife was the source of the German Lutheranism. The repeated stays in Virginia may have resulted from family involvement as visiting Lutheran pastors for the Valley of the Virginia Churches, a common practice in these years. A return to Pennsylvania followed the Virginia sojourns, with the settlement in Fayette and Greene Counties becoming permanent by 1850. The Virginia counties visited were Rockingham (John Hart), Frederick (James Curl), and Shenandoah (James Wood). These counties were all originally settled by Germans during the 1720s and 1730s, and all maintained a very high concentration of Germans well into the twentieth century. See the *Pennsylvania* and *Virginia Census* records of 1800–1870; Charles H. Glatfelter, *Pastors and People: German Lutheran and Reformed Churches in the Pennsylvania Field, 1717–1793* (Breinigsville, Pennsylvania: Pennsylvania German Society, 1980), 140, 142, and 485; and John Walter Wayland, *The German Element of the Shenandoah Valley of Virginia* (Bridgewater, Virginia: C. J. Carrier Company, 1964), 93, 95, and 113. (Another extension of the German Lutheran tradition carried through to Louis M. H. Wood. Although indifferent to religious affairs, Louis Wood wrote verse in German dialect. A comparison of the Virginia Shenandoah German dialect and the verse of Louis Wood might provide further insights. See Peterson, *John G. Haskell*, 1984, 82.)

11. "William H. Bancroft," in "Artists," typescript held at the Colorado Historical Society. The material is derived from an article in the *Colorado Springs Gazette* of August 11, 1924, that discusses the profession of "sign painting." William H. Bancroft was a landscape artist and "sign painter."

12. The Russian-German settlers grew wheat on large tracts of land, held in common during the 1880s and early 1890s. They maintained their houses and kitchen gardens separately, on individual family plots. The settlers were German by nationality but had strong ties to Russia. Their ancestors had migrated to southeastern European Russia in 1763 at the invitation of Catherine II. Russia had granted these people religious

autonomy and had allowed them to live undisturbed until imposing Russian military service in the 1870s. To avoid conscription, the German enclave moved again—to western Kansas. The land around Hays reminded the immigrants of the Russian steppes and was "treeless, level and covered with short grass." In 1878 the population of Ellis County was about 2,400, with most people living in the Russian-German communities. Mary Eloise Johannes, *A Study of the Russian-German Settlements in Ellis County, Kansas,* dissertation in social science (Washington, D.C.: The Catholic University of America Press, 1946), ix, 1, 3–4, 6, 8, 10–14, 18, 27, 29, 68, and 79.

13. Craig Miner, *West of Wichita: Settling the High Plains of Kansas, 1865–1890* (Lawrence: University Press of Kansas, 1986), 10, 163–166, 212–213, 217, and 220; Mary Ann Thompson, Kansas Room Librarian, Hays Public Library, notes characterizing the Hays climate of these years, based on archival records at the Hays Public Library, July 29, 1987.

14. "T. H. B. Wood," *Kansas Agricultural Census,* 1885, 16; "Methodist Episcopal Church," *German American Advocate,* Hays, Kansas, May 17, 1884, 1; "T. H. B. Wood," *Name Register of D.M. Vance Post No. 2 G.A.R.,* Hays City, Kansas. A Union Civil War veterans' organization, the Grand Army of the Republic (GAR) listed Wood as joining the Hays post on June 2, 1884, and transferring from it on February 2, 1891. The *Name Register* also noted T. H. B. Wood's Civil War record. The 1891 closing date probably indicates that the Wood family left Hays for Denver before the preceding winter's snowfall.

15. Miner, *West of Wichita,* 1986, 124, 128–129. Local and regional conditions were of heightened significance during these years. Severe weather in Kansas immediately affected the land-based economy but did not necessarily extend its impact outside localities. Western Kansas had bad years in 1879–1880, while Nebraska had a boom economy and milder weather patterns. Denver, for instance, was in an economic slump during the middle 1880s, while western Kansas boomed. Richard R. Brettell, *Historic Denver: The Architects and Architecture, 1858–1893* (Denver: Historic Denver, Inc., second printing 1979), 115. Western Kansas went bust during 1887–1893, while Denver enjoyed a silver-gilded prosperity.

16. "Louis M. Wood, architect," Denver City Directories, 1890, 1891, 1892, and 1893. Peterson, *John G. Haskell,* 1984, 166. Peterson notes that the Haskell and Wood partnership dissolved in May 1887, with Wood setting himself up in independent practice in Topeka.

17. Miner, *West of Wichita,* 1984, 50–51. Miner discusses how much of an impact the experience of the high plains had on children of these years. Sources include diaries, letters, and reflections left by local residents.

18. "Leadville Ice Palace," research and photograph file, Colorado Historical Society; and Fred Anderes and Ann Agranoff, *Ice Palaces* (New York: Abbeville Press, 1983).

19. "Thomas H. B. Wood, sign writer," *Denver City Directories,* 1890, 1891, 1892, and 1893. A change of residence and listed occupation occurred in 1894.

20. Brettell, *Historic Denver,* 1979, 26–30.

21. Jon A. Peterson, "The City Beautiful Movement: Forgotten Origins and Lost Meanings," in Donald A. Krueckeberg (ed.), *Introduction to Planning History in the United*

States (New Brunswick, New Jersey: Center for Urban Policy Research, 1983), 40–57. Most art clubs named themselves by their city and the term "architectural." The majority also came to life after the Columbian Exposition opened in Chicago during 1893. In 1899, Cleveland sponsored the first national convention of American architectural clubs. The Architectural League of America was organized at that meeting.

22. The authors have not reviewed *Western Architect and Building News* issue by issue to determine whether or not drawings by Louis M. H. Wood appeared in the journal during 1889–1891. Louis Wood's presentation style of these years remains unaddressed. The architect-uncle's style may have had a direct impact on the early drafting skills of Hart Wood.

23. See n. 19.

24. English artist Henry Read arrived in Denver in 1890, simultaneously with the Wood families. He taught art in the city and was thoroughly committed to the public art movement. He established the Students' School of Art in 1895, and his Artists' Club was a forerunner of the Denver Art Museum.

25. "The Denver Artists' Club," *Woman Voter and the Western Woman* 3:15 (April 25, 1895): full issue devoted to the topic; and Denver Artists' Club, *Minute Books*, vol. 1, January 1894–April 1896.

26. "Thomas H. B. Wood, janitor," *Denver City Directories*, 1894–1909. The Denver Public Library is missing the volumes for 1910–1913. By 1914, Thomas H. B. Wood is no longer listed in the directory.

27. "Wood, Hart H., with Marean and Norton," and "Wood, Thomas H. B., janitor, Franklin School," *Denver City Directory,* 1898, 1233.

Chapter 2: *Wood's Early Career*

1. Thomas J. Noel and Barbara S. Norgren, *Denver: The City Beautiful and Its Architects* (Denver: Historic Denver, Inc., 1987), 195–196, 211, and 214.

2. Frank E. Edbrooke practiced for seven years in Chicago and then worked briefly for the Union Pacific Railroad. Whether or not Hart Wood's uncle, Louis Wood, met or worked with any of the Edbrookes in Chicago during 1871–1872 is unknown. Edbrooke was a member of the GAR—the Civil War Union veterans' organization that also included Hart Wood's father, Thomas H. B. Wood. "Frank E. Edbrooke," "Artists," typescript held at the Colorado Historical Society. The material is derived from Wilbur Fiske Stone (ed.), *History of Colorado* (Chicago: S. J. Clarke, 1918–1919), vol. 2, 192.

3. "Willis Adams Marean," "Artists," typescript held at the Colorado Historical Society. The material is derived from Frank Hall, *History of the State of Colorado* (Chicago: Blakely Printing Co., 1889–1895), vol. 4, 440. Marean's father was German and his mother English—paralleling the home environment of Hart Wood.

4. Denver Artists' Club, *Minute Books*, vol. 1 (January 1894–April 1896) and vol. 2 (November 1896–May 1897). Meetings of the Denver Artists' Club during 1896–1897 occurred at 1517 Tremont, the address of Read's School of Art. Also see Doris Ostrander Dawdy, "Read, Henry (1851–1935)," in *Artists of the American West* (Chicago: Swallow Press, Inc., 1924), 191.

5. Artists' Club, *Minute Books*, vol. 2, entry of January 23, 1897. The Artists' Club eventually had a separate gallery in the Colorado Museum of Natural History, a building erected in Denver's central park for $100,000 in about 1903. Florence N. Levy (ed.), *American Art Annual* (New York: Blumenberg Press, 1903–1904), vol. 4, 187–188. The Artists' Club evolved into the Denver Art Museum in 1923. LeRoy R. Hafen (ed.), *Colorado and Its People: A Narrative and Topical History of the Centennial State* (New York: Lewis Historical Publishing Co., 1948), vol. 2, 430.

6. "Hart H. Wood," *Denver City Directories*, 1898–1903. The 1898 listing presumes that Hart Wood began working for Marean & Norton in either 1897 or 1898.

7. Frank Edbrooke retired from architectural practice in Denver in 1915 at age seventy-five. That September he capped his career by taking an automobile trip to San Francisco to see the Panama-Pacific International Exposition. *Frank E. Edbrooke* (Denver: Egan Printing Co., 1918), 42.

8. Hart Wood passed on almost none of his childhood and young-adult family history to his sons. Benton Wood, in an interview with author Karen Weitze on May 29, 1984, in Orinda, California, offered no details of his father's childhood.

9. "Wood and Simpson, Architects," *Architect and Engineer of California* 42:2 (August 1915): 109; Henry F. and Elsie Rathburn Withey, *Biographical Dictionary of American Architects (Deceased)* (Los Angeles: Hennessey and Ingalls, Inc., 1970), 291–292; Charles E. Hodges, letters to Mrs. Leland Stanford, December 27, 1901, and January 2, 1902, Stanford University Archives, SC 125. Shepley, Rutan & Coolidge had undertaken the Stanford University commission in autumn 1886, placing Hodges in charge of construction in 1891. Charles E. Hodges had arrived in Boston from London in 1888 and had immediately begun work as a draftsman for Shepley, Rutan & Coolidge. When the Boston firm became dissociated from the project in 1900, Hodges became the resident university architect, remaining in that position until 1907.

10. B. S. Allen (ed.), *California from 1769 to 1909* (San Francisco: Privately printed, 1910), 64; Ellis A. Davis (ed.), *Davis' Commercial Encyclopedia of the Pacific Southwest, California, Nevada, Utah, Arizona* (Berkeley: E. A. Davis, 1911), 220; *San Francisco City Directory*, 1903, [p.] 1948; Michael R. Corbett, *Splendid Survivors* (San Francisco: California Living Books, 1979), 106. Previously, Smith O'Brien had worked as a draftsman for Clinton Day. Architect Day had been entrusted with the design of Stanford University Memorial Church in 1891. During 1901–1902, Clinton Day and Charles E. Hodges were actively working on the church commission. Their respective draftsmen, O'Brien and Wood, must have known each other. When O'Brien left Day to become the junior partner of Frederick H. Meyer, he may have convinced Hart Wood to join the new firm. Meyer had become a practicing architect only in the late 1890s, working as junior partner of Newsom and Meyer in 1900.

11. Walter D. Bliss and William B. Faville were educated at MIT during the early 1890s. The two men then worked in the New York office of McKim, Mead and White. Bliss and Faville were originally from Northern California. Becoming friends, the men returned to San Francisco in 1898 and began a partnership that same year. Charles W. Dickey, with whom Hart Wood would later work in Hawaii, graduated from MIT in 1894.

His coursework there had overlapped that of both Bliss and Faville. Davis, *Encyclopedia*, 1911, 163, 169, and 172.

12. Remarkable coincidences existed if these people were not related. Mary Elizabeth Bliss (1837/1838–1919) and her brother John A. Bliss (1843–1924/1925) were the children of Luther and Harriet A. Bliss of Wilbraham, Massachusetts. Walter D. Bliss' father, Duane Leroy Bliss (1833–1907), was the only son of William and Mary Eliza (Barney) Bliss of Savoy, Berkshire County, Massachusetts. Luther and William were either the same age or under two years apart. Luther was born in 1807/1808; William in 1806/1807. These men may have been twins, brothers, or cousins. Their respective children may have been cousins or second cousins.

13. Peterson, *John G. Haskell*, 1984, 3, 79, 114, 217, 222, and 271; "Luther B. Bliss, Wilbraham, Hampden County," *Massachusetts Census*, 1850, 27; "William Bliss, Savoy, Berkshire County," *Massachusetts Census*, 1850, 89; "Wilbraham and Savoy, Hampden and Berkshire Counties," *Massachusetts Census*, 1820, passim; indices, *Massachusetts Census*, 1830 and 1840, passim; C. F. Curry, *California Blue Book* (Sacramento: California State Printing Office, 1903), 298 and 435; "John A. Bliss," *Oakland City Directories*, 1889–1895, passim; Justice B. Detwiler (ed.), *Who's Who in California* (San Francisco: Who's Who Publishing Co., 1928–1929), 116; "Duane Leroy Bliss," obituary, *San Francisco Examiner*, December 25, 1907, 6; and, "Walter D. Bliss," obituary, *San Francisco Chronicle*, May 10, 1956, 6.

14. *Architect and Engineer of California* articles: "To Build Temporary Hotel," 5:2 (June 1906): 70; C. Walter Tozer, "The Interior Decorative Features of the Hotel St. Francis," 16:1 (February 1909): 62–70; "Roof Garden for Hotel," 19:3 (January 1910): 61; and "Three Million Dollars for New Hotels in San Francisco," 27:3 (January 1912): 100. Hart Wood claimed the additions to the St. Francis Hotel as his design in *Architect and Engineer of California*, August 1915, 109.

15. "The Work of Charles William Dickey," *Architect and Engineer of California* 9:3 (July 1907): 35–58; Davis, *Encyclopedia*, 1911, 219.

16. "Architect Wood and Oakland Belle Will Be Married Tonight," *San Francisco Call*, November 21, 1906, 6; "Many Friends Attend Wedding," *San Francisco Chronicle*, November 22, 1906, 13.

17. "Many Friends Attend Wedding," *Chronicle*, November 22, 1906.

18. "Popular Clubman Called by Death," *San Francisco Call*, October 27, 1908, 4.

19. *Architectural Record* articles: "The New Bank of California," 19:6 (June 1906): 470–471; and untitled, 30:5 (November 1911): 440; and *Architect and Engineer of California*, untitled, 19:1 (November 1909): 52. See also *McKim, Mead and White, 1879–1915*, New York, 1973. As built, the bank was streamlined somewhat from the design appearing in *Architectural Record* in 1906. Wood claimed the Bank of California in *Architect and Engineer of California*, August 1915, 109. The Bank of California is designated a San Francisco City Landmark.

20. By 1916, Irving F. Morrow of Morrow and Garren would describe Wood's presentation style as "characterized by flatness of plane and pallor of color scheme." Morrow further commented that the method had seen "notable success in allowing the

architecture to clearly emerge through the mannerism of the presentation." Irving F. Morrow, "The Oakland Architectural Exhibition," *Architect and Engineer of California* 47:1 (October 1916): 41. Whether or not the work of the 1915–1918 years was indeed characterized by a "pallor" of color scheme is as yet impossible to know. In the one extant color photograph of a 1910 Hart Wood watercolor, the scheme is soft in tone with bright, darker pinpoints of color. By "pallor of color," Morrow may have meant *flatness* of color.

21. For example, see A. C. David, "The New San Francisco: Architectural and Social Changes Wrought by the Reconstruction," *Architectural Record* 31:160 (January 1912): 1–26. The selected Bliss and Faville buildings included the Bank of California, the Balboa Building, the Columbia Theater, the Savings Union Bank, the offices of Balfour, Guthrie and Company, and the University Club. In addition to Bliss and Faville, *Architectural Record* discussed seventeen other San Francisco architectural firms. Fifteen firms had only single-photograph illustrations, while two had double illustrations.

22. *Architect and Engineer of California* articles: "Architects Honored," 16:3 (April 1909): 85; "Honor for San Francisco Architects," 23:2 (December 1910): 100; "Competition for Portland Post Office Building," 34:2 (September 1913): 113; "Anent the Portland Postoffice [*sic*] Competition," 35:2 (December 1913): 91–94. In the Denver competition, only one other California firm was invited to submit: A. F. Rosenheim of Los Angeles. Eighteen firms were invited nationally. For Washington, D.C., twenty firms were selected to compete—all from New York, Baltimore, Chicago, and Boston, with the exception of Bliss and Faville. And for Portland (in the first competition), seven firms were invited: three from Portland, three from New York, and Bliss and Faville.

23. Hart Wood likely participated in other designs undertaken by Bliss and Faville during the 1908 to 1914 years. Notable Bliss and Faville commissions of the period that are not resolved concerning Wood's design role include a number of San Francisco buildings: the University Club (1909), the Bishop Nichols residence (1910), the London, Liverpool and Globe Insurance Company (1910), reconstruction of the Rialto Building (1910), reconstruction of the Occidental Hotel (1910), the Eastman Kodak Building (1911), the Balboa Building (1912), and the Flood Mansion (1913). Also falling into this group is the multibuilding Women's Republic Community in Atascadero, California, an important Arts and Crafts utopian town in design beginning in 1913. *Architect and Engineer of California*, passim, 1908–1914; B. J. S. Cahill, "The Work of Bliss and Faville," *Architect and Engineer of California* 35:3 (January 1914): 47–56. The firm also entered both the Oakland (1910) and the San Francisco (1912) City Hall competitions, as well as undertaking several buildings in Oakland. In particular, the Liverpool, London and Globe Insurance Company Building is most likely Wood's work. A published black and white photograph of a watercolor presentation drawing can be from almost no other hand. See *Architect and Engineer of California* 23:3 (January 1911): 42. The University Club (1909) and the Balboa Building (1912) also are possibilities.

24. August G. Headman, "A Review of the San Francisco Architectural Club's Exhibition," *Architect and Engineer of California* 19:1 (November 1909): 53. Interestingly enough, Bliss and Faville were disqualified from the Oakland City Hall competition due to their use of color, which violated the rules of the competition. See "Oakland City Hall

Competition," *Architect and Engineer of California* 20:3 (April 1910): 90; also, *Architect and Engineer of California* 21:2 (June 1910): 48.

25. *Architect and Engineer of California* articles: "Ransome Concrete Company Awarded Contract for Columbia Theater," 15:1 (November 1908): 109; and C. W. Whitney, "The Columbia Theater Building," 15:3 (January 1909): 43–44. San Francisco Architectural Club, *Fifth Exhibition Yearbook* (San Francisco: C. A. Murdock Co., 1909).

26. "Ransome Concrete Company," *Architect and Engineer of California* (November 1908): 109. The Columbia Theater, known as the Geary by the middle 1980s, is listed in the National Register of Historic Places and is designated a San Francisco City Landmark.

27. *Architect and Engineer of California* articles: "Savings Union to Build," 17:2 (June 1909): 112ff.; "Savings Union Bank and Trust Company," 30:3 (October 1912): 56. *McKim, Mead and White*, 1973.

28. *Architect and Engineer of California* articles: "Weather Beaten Tile," 20:1 (February 1910): 113; and "Entrance Detail, Children's Hospital, San Francisco," 30:2 (September 1912): 61.

29. *Architect and Engineer of California* articles: "Bliss and Faville Busy," 22:2 (September 1910): 97; January 1911: 69, 74, and 79; "San Francisco's Splendid Masonic Temple," 25:1 (May 1911): 119. Thomas Plant, Plant Contractors, San Francisco, owned a color photograph of the watercolor presentation drawing in the middle 1980s. Mr. Plant was a co-owner of the building for a number of years. The current location of the watercolor is unknown. The published *Architect and Engineer of California* photograph of the watercolor (January 1911) is cropped to remove Wood's signature, again giving official credit only to Bliss and Faville. Thomas Plant also owned a partial set of oversized ink-on-linen drawings for the temple. Of these, the following are initialed "H.W.": #24, "Eastern Star Lodge Room," 41.5 by 41.5 inches; #100, multiple interior and exterior details, 56.5 by 42 inches; #104, "Main Entrance," 43.25 by 30 inches; and #121, "Eastern Star Lodge Room," 29.5 x 41.5 inches. Among the linens surviving, those initialed "H.W." are the ones with elaborate detailing. Others include simple elevations, floor plans, sections, and heating and electrical plans. From the initials of the other draftsmen working on the project between 1910 and 1913, it appears that the Bliss and Faville staff consisted of about fourteen individuals. The extant collection contains fifty-three linens.

30. "View Masonic Temple," *Architect and Engineer of California* 35:2 (December 1913): 113.

31. Site visit, September 12, 1984. Special thanks to Fred Lee, Plant Contractors, for his arrangements. The Masonic Temple was in the final stages of renovation at the time of the visit.

32. *Architect and Engineer of California* articles: "Oakland Architectural Club," 23:1 (November 1910): 101; and "Annual Meeting of Oakland Architectural Association," 28:2 (March 1912): 101. Wood's founding of the Oakland Architectural Club may reflect his memory of the Denver Architectural Sketch Club and the Denver Artists' Club of twenty years earlier. These self-formed art and architectural organizations provided critical education for many American draftsmen and young architects, ca. 1886–1920.

33. The participation of other prominent East Bay architects in the Oakland clubs, such as Bernard Maybeck and Julia Morgan, remains undetermined.

34. *Architect and Engineer of California* articles: "Architectural Exhibit for Oakland," 45:3 (June 1916): 108; "Oakland Architectural Exhibit," 46:2 (August 1916): 109; Morrow, "Oakland" (October 1916): 39–70; and Alameda County Society of Architects, *Yearbook: Exhibition of October 2 through 10, 1916* (San Francisco: Taylor and Taylor, 1916).

35. Hart Wood took the exam on January 31, 1911. The State of California issued the certificate on February 3, 1911: Certificate 156B. California State Archives, Sacramento.

36. Special thanks to George M. Keefer, owner of the Hart Wood house in the middle 1980s, for his consideration in permitting interviews, site visits, and photographs. Thanks also to Mrs. Miles for her help in researching the house. Karen Weitze interviews with George M. Keefer, August 31, 1984, and with Mrs. Miles, August 31, 1984. Site visits, August 31 and September 13, 1984.

37. Louis C. Mullgardt, "Panama-Pacific Exposition at San Francisco," *Architectural Record* 37:3 (March 1915): 192–228.

38. W. B. Faville, "Phases of Panama-Pacific International Exposition Architecture," *American Architect* 107:2037 (January 6, 1915): 1–7 and plates; B. J. S. Cahill, "A Criticism of Some of the Work Shown at the Annual Exhibition of San Francisco Architectural Club," *Architect and Engineer of California* 32:3 (April 1913): 68 and 75; Donald McLaren, "Landscape Gardening at the Exposition," the *Architect* 10:1 (July 1915): 12–23.

39. *Architect and Engineer of California* articles: Cahill, "A Criticism of Some of the Work" (April 1913): 68; "New Firm of Architects," 42:1 (July 1915): 133; "Wood and Simpson, Architects" (August 1915): 109. Wood described his work on the Panama-Pacific International Exposition as the "main group of buildings."

40. William L. Woollett, "Color in Architecture at the Panama-Pacific Exposition," *Architectural Record* 37:5 (May 1915): 438.

41. "The Portal of the Palace of Varied Industries," *Pacific Coast Architect* 7:3 (May 1914): 95–96; Woollett, "Color," *Architectural Record* (May 1915): 438; *Architectural Record* 38:5 (November 1915): 562–574; Ralph S. Fanning, "Consideration of Color in Architectural Design," *American Architect* 109:2109 (May 10, 1916): 310–311.

42. McLaren, "Landscape," the *Architect* (July 1915): 12–23; Frank Morton Todd, *The Story of the Panama-Pacific International Exposition* (New York: G. P. Putnam's Sons, 1921), 310–311; Faville, "Phases," *American Architect* 107:2039 (January 6, 1915): 7. American Institute of Architects, "Nomination for Fellowship by the Hawaii Chapter," AIA Archives, Washington, D.C.

43. "Personal," *Architect and Engineer of California* 38:3 (October 1914): 117. The journal noted, "Walter Wood, who has been Bliss and Faville's head draftsman for a number of years, is now a member of the staff of Louis [*sic*] Hobart." "Walter" must be "Hart." "Louis" should be "Lewis."

44. Articles in *Architect and Engineer of California* 38:3 (October 1914): "War Will Affect Architects' Supplies," 134; "How One Architectural Firm Meets the Slack Times," 101. The volume of business mentioned makes it extremely likely that the firm referenced was Bliss and Faville.

45. Davis, *Encyclopedia*, 212; George F. M. Nellist, *Pan-Pacific Who's Who* (Hono-

lulu: Honolulu Star-Bulletin, 1941), 317; *Pacific Coast Architect* 7:1 (March 1914): 40; "California," *Pacific Coast Architect* 7:2 (August 1914): 77; Louis Christian Mullgardt, "The Architecture of Mr. Lewis Hobart," *Architect and Engineer of California* 42:2 (August 1915): 38–89.

46. *Pacific Coast Architect* articles: "California," 7:3 (September 1914): 121; and "Oregon," 8:4 (October 1914): 162. Also Alameda County Society of Architects, *Yearbook*, 1916, and "Architect Hobart in Washington," *Architect and Engineer of California* 44:2 (February 1916): 109. The watercolors for the Portland Post Office and the University of California Hospital were both signed but clipped as published. The watercolor style resembles Wood's. Publication only as watercolors, not photographs, as late as October 1916, suggests that both commissions had run into trouble. At best, construction remained uncompleted for both buildings. A Hobart watercolor entitled "Study for a Church, San Francisco," published in *Architect and Engineer of California* 42:1 (July 1915): 97, as well as in the *Yearbook* of 1916, may also be Wood's.

Chapter 3: *Wood and Simpson*

1. *Architect and Engineer of California* articles: "New Firm of Architects," 42:1 (July 1915): 133; and "Wood and Simpson, Architects," 42:2 (August 1915): 109; "Current Notes and Comments," the *Architect* 10:6 (December 1915): 278.

2. Llewellyn B. Dutton had studied and worked in Chicago, 1881–1903, with William LeBaron Jenny, Cobb and Frost, and Daniel H. Burnham. In 1903, he went to California in the interests of Burnham. After 1906, Dutton set up practice for himself. With the opening of Dutton's firm, Horace G. Simpson became head designer, arriving in San Francisco that same year. Simpson was a graduate of MIT. He had studied in Europe on the Rotch Traveling Scholarship and had been employed as a designer with Cass Gilbert and Guy Lowell. Horace G. Simpson lived in Berkeley, 1912–1917. While with Dutton's firm, he had worked on the First Trust and Savings Bank, Oakland; the competition plans for the San Francisco City Hall; and the Holt Manufacturing Pavilion at the Panama-Pacific International Exposition. Davis, *Encyclopedia*, 214; see also chapter 2, n. 45. For Simpson's residency, see the *Oakland, Berkeley, and Alameda County City Directories*, as well as the *San Francisco City Directories*, 1913–1918.

3. Horace G. Simpson took the exam on November 24, 1914. The State of California issued his certificate to practice architecture on December 1, 1914. Certificate 243B, California State Archives, Sacramento. "S.F. Chapter, AIA," the *Architect* 10:1 (July 1915): 42. Hart Wood was never a member of the San Francisco chapter. Perhaps his lack of formal architectural education and travel kept him from the membership rolls, or perhaps he chose not to seek membership. All of the architects for and with whom he worked during 1902–1918 were members: Hodges, Meyer, O'Brien, Bliss, Faville, Hobart, Simpson, and Dickey.

4. *Architect and Engineer of California* articles: H. G. Simpson, "The Skyline of San Francisco—An Opportunity," 45:3 (June 1916): 62–68; "Santa Fe Leases Skyscraper," 45:3 (June 1916): 108; "More About Santa Fe Building," 46:1 (July 1916): 109; and "The Santa Fe Building, San Francisco," 48:2 (February 1917): 55–57. Additional plates:

the *Architect* 14:5 (November 1917): plates 73–78. Also, site visit by Karen Weitze, September 12, 1984.

5. *Architect and Engineer of California* articles: "Five-Story Apartments," 44:3 (March 1916): 109; "An Apartment House Designed in the Colonial Style," 48:2 (February 1917): 38–42; and J. F. Dunn, "Apartment Houses," 58:3 (September 1919): 78–79.

6. Karen J. Weitze, "Utopian Place Making: The Built Environment in Arts and Crafts California," in Kenneth R. Trapp (ed.), *The Arts and Crafts Movement in California: Living the Good Life* (New York: Abbeville Press, 1993), 55–87; and Karen J. Weitze, "Midwest to California: The Planned Arts and Crafts Community," in Bert Denker (ed.), *The Substance of Style: Perspectives on the American Arts and Crafts Movement* (Hanover and London: University Press of New England, 1996), 447–469.

7. *Architect and Engineer of California* articles: "A Model Civic Center for the Women's Republic Community, Atascadero," 31:1 (November 1913): 69–74; "A Model City," 41:1 (May 1915): 109; and "More Buildings for Atascadero Colony," 46:3 (September 1916): 127. The colony was never completed to the full scale of the original plans. See n. 28.

8. Horace G. Simpson, articles in *Architect and Engineer of California*: "An English Cottage at the Exposition," 43:1 (October 1915): 44–48; "Residence Sub-Division—Its Relation to Urban Development and to Architecture," 43:3 (December 1915): 38–46. The Piedmont mansion was likely a commission that fell through before construction. In talking with a number of local residents, as well as searching the appropriate neighborhoods, no house resembling the published design—or knowledge of such a residence—has surfaced.

9. Wood and Simpson may have been familiar with the work of Lutyens and Voysey through both English and American professional journals. Other well-circulated sources, such as M. B. Adams' *Modern Cottage Architecture* of 1912, also included representative work by both masters. Critics recommended Adams' book in *Architectural Record* in December 1912.

10. C. Matlock Price, "Notes on the Varied Work of Willis Polk," *Architectural Record* 34:6 (December 1913): 565.

11. The two distinct approaches to the planning of small cities continued during the next half decade. Beaux Arts town cores were even coupled with rambling, picturesque outlying residential tracts. The civic center designed for Hampstead Garden Suburb by Lutyens (1908) is a major example of the merger of the garden city of Ebenezer Howard with the City Beautiful. In the United States, the design of towns for private industries and for selected federal agencies, 1915–1918, also saw such partnerships. See n. 27.

12. The Burlingame commission remains a puzzling one. *Architect and Engineer of California* published the numbered sketches of Horace G. Simpson, dated September 1915, in February 1916 accompanying one of Simpson's articles. The journal published the presentation drawing by Hart Wood, dated 1915, the following month—with one of Simpson's essays. See n. 15. Several possible connections between Lyon and Hoag and Hart Wood may have stimulated the undertaking of the commission. In 1911, Bliss and Faville designed the W. S. Oliver residence. Oliver was a member of the Lyon and Hoag firm. In addition, Lewis P. Hobart was known for his residential work on the San Francisco peninsula, including major mansions in the Burlingame–Hillsborough–San Marco corridor.

Hobart had several of these residences in their completion stages while Wood worked for him. See "San Francisco Architects Busy," *Architect and Engineer of California* 24:3 (April 1911): 99; *San Mateo News-Leader*, July 1915–September 1916, passim (especially May 5, 1916: 2 and July 18, 1916: 2); *San Francisco Chronicle*, April 20, 1929: 5; Frank M. Stanger, *Peninsula Community Book* (San Mateo: A. H. Cawston, 1946), 388–389; L. F. Byington, *History of San Francisco* (Chicago and San Francisco: S. J. Clarke, 1931), vol. 2, 389–391.

13. "English Homes Will Be Built in Burlingame," *San Mateo News-Leader*, May 5, 1916: 3.

14. In 1916, the population of Burlingame was about four thousand. Builders had developed several small suburban enclaves in the town, but the overall number of residences was still under a hundred. In driving the appropriate tracts of Burlingame twice and in checking with the San Mateo County Recorder's office, Weitze did not find a cluster of houses fitting the Wood and Simpson proposed design. Of the probable subdivisions, that of Easton would have been most likely. Philip W. Alexander and Charles P. Hamm, *History of San Mateo County* (Burlingame: P. W. Alexander and C. P. Hamm, 1916), 54 and 65.

15. Wood and Simpson published two designs for schools in *Architect and Engineer of California* 44:1 (January 1916): 98–99. In addition, Simpson wrote two more articles for the journal. See *Architect and Engineer of California*: "The Suburban Home—Its Design and Setting," 44:2 (February 1916): 39–45; and "The Landscape Architecture and Planting of Suburban Residence Districts," 44:3 (March 1916): 72–78.

16. The Holt Pavilion is included in Todd's *Story of the Panama-Pacific International Exposition* of 1921 in vol. 4, pages 262–263.

17. Simpson, "An English Cottage," *Architect and Engineer of California* (October 1915): 44–48. The Panama-Pacific International Exposition closed on December 4, 1915. During 1916 and 1917, a few of the fair buildings were relocated. Prominent among these were the California, Oregon, Ohio, Wisconsin, and Siam Buildings. The Palace of Fine Arts (Maybeck) and the Hawaiian Building (Dickey) remained on the exposition site. "Making Use of Exposition Buildings," *Architect and Engineer of California* 50:2 (August 1917): 110.

18. Arthur Upham Pope and Phyllis Ackerman purchased the Holt Pavilion in about early 1916, intending on making it a permanent home. Professor Pope taught at the University of California–Berkeley from 1911 through 1917. He then accepted a position at Amherst College, later returning to San Francisco as the director of the California Art Museum. During his career, Professor Pope was advisory curator for several American museums and published prolifically between 1917 and 1965. Phyllis Ackerman also wrote professionally. Pope and Ackerman were intense individuals, active in art, teaching, and community issues. They lived in their Wood and Simpson–designed Berkeley house only about a year. Upon returning to San Francisco in the 1920s, the couple lived on the other side of San Francisco Bay. Detwiler, *Who's Who in California, 1928–29*, 1929, 243; *San Francisco Chronicle*, October 3, 1915, 27; George Malcolm Stratton and Chester H. Rowell Papers and Phoebe A. Hearst Letters, Bancroft Library, Berkeley.

19. The earliest of seventeen extant blueprints for the Pope-Ackerman house date to

April 6, 1916. In all likelihood, Professors Pope and Ackerman planned the residence for a site in Northbrae, a self-contained suburb on the northern edge of Berkeley. For whatever reason, however, the couple abandoned their plans for the initial site. After a lull of several months, men relocated the house farther to the north and east, in the more exclusive Berkeley suburb of Cragmont. *Architect and Engineer of California* articles: "English House for Northbrae," 45:2 (May 1916): 121; and "New Residence for Cragmont," 46:1 (July 1916): 108.

20. *Architect and Engineer of California* articles: Morrow, "Oakland" (October 1916): 39; Frederick Jennings, "Domestic Architecture in California," 49:2 (May 1917): 48–56; Kenneth Saunders (a University of California professor and then owner of the Pope house), "High Acres: An English Cottage in Berkeley, California," *House Beautiful* 57:4 (April 1925): 365–367; Sanborn Insurance Company, "605 Woodmont Avenue," *Berkeley*, vol. 4 (1929): 458 (map). John McLaren's *Gardening in California: Landscape and Flower* (San Francisco: A. M. Robertson, 1909) may have influenced Hart Wood.

21. Site visits and interviews with owner Gall Fogerty by Karen Weitze, September 3 and 12, 1984. *American Architect* ran a series of articles on Tudor domestic interior details during 1915–1918 that demonstrated the archaeologically correct qualities of Simpson's design for the interior of the Holt Pavilion (1914). *American Architect* articles: "The Paneled Room," 107:2061 (June 23, 1915): 399–403; "English Details, No. 1–11," 107:2162–2208 (May 30, 1917–April 17, 1918): passim.

22. *American Architect* first mentioned the competition for the San Francisco State Building in March 1916. See: *American Architect* 109:2098 (March 8, 1916); 109:2112 (June 14, 1916); 110:2136 (November 29, 1916); 110:2138 (December 13, 1916); and 111:2150 (March 7, 1917). For details on the contest, see the *Architect*: "Architectural Competition," 12:6 (December 1916): 396; "Minutes of San Francisco Chapter," 13:1 (January 1917): 60; 13:3 (March 1917): plates. Also see B. J. S. Cahill, "Plans for the State Building on the San Francisco Civic Center," *Architect and Engineer of California* 48:3 (March 1917): 39–62; and "San Francisco State Building Extracts from Program of Competition," *American Architect* 112:2172 (August 8, 1917): 109–110. The Building Material Exhibit displayed the drawings of the semifinalists in San Francisco. The State Building was to be incorporated in Civic Center Square. Entirely Beaux Arts in design, plan, and urban arrangement, the San Francisco State Building complemented an auditorium (John Galen Howard, Frederick H. Meyer, John Reid Jr., 1914), city hall (Bakewell and Brown, 1915), and the public library (George W. Kelham, 1916). Adjacent to the library was the future site of the opera house. The eight placing architects each received $1,000. The winner was to get 6 percent of the total cost of the building, excluding furniture.

23. "State Building," *Architect and Engineer of California* 48:3 (March 1917): 62; the *Architect* articles: William Mooser, "State Building Competition," 13:4 (April 1917): 265–267; and "San Francisco State Building," 15:6 (June 1918): 350, 375–376.

24. Charles W. Dickey organized the Oakland exhibition. (See chapter 2, n. 34.) "Alameda County Society of Architects" is interpreted as an informal name given to those architects living in the East Bay. The exhibition included architects from San Francisco as well, and the opening pages of the catalogue listed the membership of the San Francisco

AIA chapter. Wood and Simpson had three watercolors displayed in the show: the Pope-Ackerman residence, a study for a bank building, and a design for a church in Stockton (east of the Bay Area in the San Joaquin Delta).

25. *Architect and Engineer of California* listed "E. L. Simpson" among its twenty-five editors in March 1917. By June, the entry had become "Horace G. Simpson." Presumably the first and second "Simpsons" were the same person. Documentation of the journal's editors continued through 1920. In 1921, *Architect and Engineer of California* no longer separately listed its editors.

26. The Pacific Electric Metals Company, like many war-related industries, did not survive the armistice of November 1918. In a situation similar to the ownership of the Pope-Ackerman residence, the Bay Point subdivision was only briefly associated with its original patron. By late 1931, Bay Point had renamed itself Port Chicago, and in 1942 the town became the location for a naval magazine within the jurisdiction of Mare Island. During World War II, Port Chicago was the principal West Coast shipping point for munitions. On July 17, 1944, two explosions triggered 3.5 million pounds of stored munitions. The blast killed over 322 people. Another 390 individuals were among the injured. All buildings in Port Chicago were damaged, with reports as far away as Oakland. The possibility of another major accident continued to haunt Port Chicago during the remainder of the 1940s, 1950s, and 1960s. To secure the property, the navy purchased the entire town site and an adjacent 27,000 acres by the close of 1969. In the middle 1980s, the land was vacant, except for a few military structures. George C. Collier, *A Narrative History of Contra Costa County* (El Cerrito: Super Print, 1983), 141–148.

27. *Martinez Standard* articles: "Ferro-Sillicon [*sic*] Factory Soon," July 18, 1917, 1; "$50,000 for Bay Point Building Boom," July 26, 1917, 1; "Bay Point a Center of Building Boom," September 7, 1917, 1; "Bay Point Ready for Business January 1," September 15, 1917, 1; "Bay Point Plant Will Be Fifty-Five Acres," September 19, 1917, 1; and "Bay Point is on the Map with Big Plans," October 17, 1917, 1. Also, "Giant Industry at Bay Point," *Byron Times*, September 7, 1917, 1; "Building Garden City for Workmen," *San Francisco Chronicle*, September 29, 1917, 11; "Contract Awarded Bay Point," *Building and Engineering News*, August 29, 1917, 6 (Bancroft Library); "Planning Numerous Dwellings," *Architect and Engineer of California* 50:3 (September 1917): 108; "Building News," *American Architect* 113:2182 (October 17, 1917): 8 and the closing pages following 292.

28. American rethinking of the industrial town, 1913–1918, fell into three distinct phases: the tentative yet elaborate model towns of 1913–1916 (see n. 7); the clusters of newly principled worker houses dependent on adjacent older urban centers, 1916–1917; and the federally aided towns-in-the-suburbs of 1918. Lawrence Veiller—who had begun his reform career as a participant in the scientific housing movement in New York City during the 1890s, and who also had helped to establish the National Housing Association in 1910—best chronicled the appearance of the World War I new towns. See: Lawrence Veiller, "Industrial Housing," a four-part series in *American Architect*, January 17, 1917–March 7, 1917, passim; "Industrial Housing Developments in America," a six-part series in *Architectural Record*, March–August 1918, passim; and Southern Pine Asso-

ciation, *Homes for Workmen: A Presentation of Leading Examples of Industrial Community Development* (New Orleans: Southern Pine Association, 1919).

29. "Personal," *Architect and Engineer of California* 51:3 (December 1917): 107; and "Current Notes," the *Architect* 14:6 (December 1917): 402. The success of Wood and Simpson can be evaluated in monetary terms. During the first sixteen months of the firm's life, the partnership garnered no income. The firm's first two projects, the Pope-Ackerman residence and the Randolph Apartments, yielded about $2,700 for each partner. (The Pope house was a $10,000 job; the apartments about an $80,000 job.) After four more dry months, Wood and Simpson received their percentage for the Santa Fe Building, as well as their $1,000 prize for a semifinalist place in the San Francisco State Building competition: about $5,000 each. (The Santa Fe Building was about a $150,000 job.) The firm faced another empty period of about ten months before being paid between $5,000 and $6,000 each for Bay Point. Where no exact figures exist, estimates were determined on a 6 percent basis, looking at projects of a comparable size, type, and location. For Bay Point, Wood and Simpson's percentage is derived from a gross project size of $165,000 to $200,000, based on unit costs of $3,000 to $3,500 for fifty-five houses. During their thirty-month partnership, Hart Wood and Horace G. Simpson probably grossed about $13,000 to $14,000 each. Their actual profits (after paying the firm's expenses) were certainly less.

30. *Architect and Engineer of California* articles: "Plans Being Prepared," 53:1 (April 1918): 131; "Houses for Walter H. Leimert Company," 55:3 (December 1918): 48 (photographs).

31. Hart Wood, "The Significance of the Housing Crisis," the *Architect* 11:1 (January 1918): 51–53; *Architect and Engineer of California* 54:1 (July 1918): passim; Veiller, "Industrial Housing Developments in America: Part I and II," *Architectural Record*, March 1918, 232–236, and April 1918, 344–359. For the tracts financed by the United States Shipping Board appropriations, see *American Architect*, May 15, 1918; also February–December 1918, passim. Hart Wood worked in a shipbuilding plant for about a year before going to Hawaii with Charles W. Dickey. Benton Wood, interview with Karen Weitze, May 29, 1984.

32. Metson, a San Franciscan who had made his fortune as a mining lawyer, had been a noteworthy figure involved in San Francisco park planning and had served on the Yosemite Park Commission. The lawyer had purchased a thousand acres on Union Island in 1916. He, like other wealthy San Franciscans, was anticipating the parceling of the 23,000-acre island into small farms. Union Island was to be an oversized subdivision of gentlemen farmers who would commute to San Francisco. Not surprisingly, also managing a substantial tract of the acreage was the San Francisco real estate firm Lyon and Hoag, the developers of Burlingame. Hart Wood may have known Metson through his San Francisco and park planning ties, or Lyon and Hoag may have recommended him to Metson after the Wood and Simpson subdivision project for Burlingame. Press Reference Library, *Notables of the Southwest* (Los Angeles: Los Angeles Examiner, 1912), 363; Franklin Harper, *Who's Who on the Pacific Coast* (Los Angeles: Harper Publishing Co., 1913), 396; George H. Meyer, Arthur H. Johnson, and D. Wooster Taylor, *Municipal Blue*

Book of San Francisco 1915, 130; and *Byron Times*, Special Development Editions, 1916, 1918, 1920–1921, 1928–1929, 1930–1931, passim.

33. Hart Wood, "Farm Buildings," the *Architect* 16:2 (January 1918): 96–97; and Alfred Hopkins, *Modern Farm Buildings* (New York: Robert M. McBride and Co., rev. ed., 1916).

34. John J. Klaber, "The Grouping of Farm Buildings: Examples from the Work of Alfred Hopkins," *Architectural Record* 37:4 (April 1915): 340–359. Also see *American Architect* articles: Alfred Hopkins, "The Modern Farm Building," 109:2090 (January 12, 1916): 17–25 and plates; "Improving the Farmer's Surroundings," 114:2237 (November 6, 1918): 549–550 and plates; 114:2238 (November 13, 1918): 571 and 574; and 114:2240 (November 27, 1918): 660.

35. "Farm Buildings," *Architect and Engineer of California* 54:3 (September 1918): 115.

36. *Architect and Engineer of California* articles: "Good Advice," 53:2 (May 1918): 127; "A Thinking Spell for Architects," 53:2 (May 1918): 99; "Architects' Drive," 54:1 (July 1918): 114; and "The Profession and the Building Trades Should Plan Now for the Future," 55:2 (November 1918): 111.

37. "Personal," *Architect and Engineer of California* 54:3 (September 1918): 113.

38. "The Work of Charles William Dickey," *Architect and Engineer of California* 9:3 (July 1907): 35–58.

39. The State of California issued Dickey's certificate to practice architecture on August 4, 1904. Certificate 29B, California State Archives, Sacramento.

40. "Personal," *Architect and Engineer of California* 56:2 (February 1919): 114.

41. Charles Dickey had previously partnered with Walter D. Reed as Dickey and Reed (1903) and Jonathon J. Donovan as Donovan and Dickey (1916). "Oakland Architects Form Partnership," *California Architect and Engineer* 46:1 (July 1916): 107.

42. *Architect and Engineer of California* articles: "Dickey and Wood, Architects, Honolulu," 57:1 (April 1919): 115; "Greek Theater for Honolulu," 58:2 (August 1919): 102–103; and "Goes to Honolulu," 59:1 (October 1919): 120.

43. "Pride of His Profession," *Honolulu Advertiser*, February 24, 1957, 3.

Chapter 4: *Hawaii*

1. For commentary on turn of the century prosperity and building activity, see *Pacific Commercial Advertiser*, "Hawaiian Prosperity," January 1, 1902, 4, and "The Story of the Decade," January 3, 1903.

2. See Thomas Thrum's *Hawaiian Annual* for the years 1929 and 1931, page 13 of each volume, the table, "Building Construction Values, Honolulu."

Chapter 5: *Early Work in Hawaii*

1. C. W. Dickey had introduced an early version of the Spanish Mission style to Hawaii with William Irwin's Waikiki residence, constructed in 1899. H. L. Kerr adopted a Mediterranean form for the Methodist Church at Beretania and Victoria streets (1910), and Ripley and Reynolds did likewise in the YMCA at the corner of Hotel and Alakea

(1911). However, it would not be until the 1920s that the form attained great popularity in Hawaii. For information on the Herman Von Holt residence, see *Architect and Engineer*, February 1927, and the *Honolulu Advertiser*, June 23, 1920, section 2: 2; July 28, 1920, section 2: 2; August 4, 1920, section 2: 2; and April 13, 1921, section 2: 4.

2. For information on the Francis Ii Brown residence, see the *Honolulu Star-Bulletin*, January 26, 1921, 10; the *Honolulu Advertiser*, April 13, 1921, section 2: 4, and October 10, 1921, Homes Section, 2; *Architect and Engineer*, February 1927; and Catherine Jones Richards, "Hawaiian Homes," *Paradise of the Pacific* (December 1933): 66–68.

3. *Honolulu Star-Bulletin*, January 26, 1921, 10.

4. The Lewers and Cooke advertisement of March 15, 1931, which appeared in the *Honolulu Advertiser*, with its facile description of a Waikiki residence as "distinctly Hawaiian in treatment," well discloses the common acceptance of a Hawaiian style of architecture by the end of the 1920s. A further indication of the public discussion of the concept of regional design is an article Honolulu architect Robert Miller wrote refuting the idea of a Hawaiian style of architecture. See the *Honolulu Star-Bulletin*, December 12, 1925, 5.

5. *Honolulu Star-Bulletin*, September 22, 1920, 12.

6. *Honolulu Star-Bulletin*, February 9, 1921, 12.

7. *Honolulu Star-Bulletin*, July 26, 1922, 13.

8. For information on the First Church of Christ Scientist, see the *Honolulu Advertiser*, January 11, 1923, 6; January 1, 1924, 4; and January 4, 1925, 4; and Thomas Thrum's *Hawaiian Annual* for 1924, 160, and for 1925, 30.

9. The Church of Christ Science had a profound influence on ecclesiastical design in Hawaii. Ralph Adams Cram would follow Wood's example and open up the nave to Central Union Church in 1925 with double doorways traversing both side walls, and Wood would open the nave of the Chinese Christian Church in a similar manner. However, it would not be until the 1950s that Wood's use of side lanais and doors would become a standard part of the architectural vocabulary for houses of worship. A number of Christian churches from this period—including Alfred Preis' United Methodist Church, Law and Wilson's Holy Nativity Episcopal Church in Aina Haina and Kalihi Union Church—all incorporated lava rock in their walls as well. Other examples of side lanai churches that did not use lava rock in their design include Kenneth Sato's deco-inspired Waiola Congregational Church in Lahaina and Edwin Bauer's modern adaptation of the Gothic Revival in St. Elizabeth's Episcopal Church. Buddhist architecture during the 1950s and 1960s would also incorporate this idea, as may be observed in the Soto Zen Mission in Nuuanu and the Waipahu Hongwanji.

10. *Honolulu Star-Bulletin*, April 21, 1920, 8.

11. For information on the Home Electric, see the *Honolulu Advertiser*, October 27, 1920, section 3: 1; November 10, 1920, section 2: 2; May 11, 1921, section 2: 4; May 18, 1921, section 2: 2–3; and May 25, 1921, 6. Dr. Nathaniel Benyas purchased this house in 1921 and resided there until 1942. For the George R. Ward residence, see the *Honolulu Star-Bulletin*, March 1, 1924, section 2: 1.

12. For information on the Rudolph Bukeley residence, see the *Honolulu Advertiser*, March 22, 1922, 9.

Chapter 6: *Wood Leads the Hawaiian Regional Architecture Movement*

1. *Honolulu Star-Bulletin*, April 21, 1920, 8.

2. Loraine E. Kuck, "Pioneering in Architecture in Hawaii," *Architect and Engineer* (February 1927): 59; for other commentary on the Morgan house, see *Honolulu Advertiser*, June 15, 1924, 15, and March 29, 1925, 12.

3. For information on the Gideon Van Poole residence, see *Honolulu Advertiser*, July 27, 1924, 13.

4. *Honolulu Advertiser*, June 15, 1924, 15.

5. Loraine Kuck, "Pioneering in Architecture in Hawaii," *Architect and Engineer* (February 1927): 59.

6. Loraine Kuck, "Architecture in Hawaii," *Pacific Coast Architect* (January 1927): 9; *House and Garden* 51:3 (March 1927), also published the Cooke residence. Also see *Honolulu Advertiser*, August 17, 1924, 13.

7. *Pacific Commercial Advertiser*, May 14, 1908, 10.

8. The last two mentioned sources by Ogawa were loaned to Wood by Fred Ashley of the San Francisco architectural firm Ashley, Evers & Hayes. These were borrowed when the Alexander & Baldwin Building was under design. See letters dated February 29, 1928, with regard to Siren's three-volume *Imperial Palaces of Peking*. Hart Wood on November 7, 1928, wrote to Miss Ethelwyn Castle, "I have a set in my office and have found them a source of considerable inspiration."

9. *Honolulu Advertiser*, April 26, 1931, 18.

10. The "treasure house in the Pacific" description was a gem gleaned from the Pan-Pacific Union's promotion of Hawaii as "the cross-roads of the Pacific." This quoted description appeared in the *Honolulu Star-Bulletin*, February 19, 1929, 11–12, as do all others on the Gump Building, unless otherwise noted. For further information on the building, see Loraine E. Kuck, "Adapting Oriental Architecture to American Needs," *Architect and Engineer* (October 1929): 35–47.

11. Carol Green Wilson, *Gump's Treasure Trade* (New York: Thomas Y. Crowell Co., 1949), 168.

12. July 9, 1928, Hardie Phillip letter to Hart Wood.

13. November 16, 1928, Hart Wood letter to Hardie Phillip.

14. *Honolulu Star-Bulletin*, February 19, 1929, 8.

15. *Honolulu Advertiser*, June 16, 1929, 11, described the church. It is also covered in Loraine E. Kuck, "Adapting Oriental Architecture to American Needs," *Architect and Engineer* (October 1929): 35–47. The latter noted Wood's use of "plaster lattice" and found that "the insertion of a grill of plaster in a plain stucco wall . . . offers one of the most charming forms of decoration imaginable." Wood appears to have developed this decorative element from illustrations of Chinese masonry-screened windows. Following his introduction of the form to Hawaii in the Mrs. C. M. Cooke residence, Wood repeatedly used it in other jobs, including the Dr. Morgan residence, the S. & G. Gump Building, the Chinese Christian Church, Honolulu Hale, and a number of Board of Water Supply pumping stations. It became a familiar form in Hawaiian design with other

architects, such as Hardie Phillip, Robert Miller, C. W. Dickey, and Harry K. Stewart, incorporating it into their designs, as exemplified by the Territorial Tax Office Building, C. Brewer, Kamehameha Schools, the U.S. Immigration Station, and the Honolulu Academy of Arts. The Territorial Tax Office Building's screens are undoubtedly directly influenced by Wood, as James Tomita, a former draftsman in Wood's office, was primarily responsible for the design of that building.

16. A letter from Dickey to Wood dated June 1, 1928, indicates the financial arrangements of the partnership. Prior to August 15, 1927, they shared the expenses and profits of their partnership at a ratio of Wood one-third, Dickey two-thirds. After August 15, 1927, the ratio changed to Wood 40 percent, Dickey 60 percent.

17. A letter from Jesse E. Stanton of Gladding, McBean dated December 17, 1928, to Hart Wood noted Mr. Trapet's greatest inspiration for this tile work was gleaned from Owen Jones' *Examples of Chinese Ornament* (London: S and T Gilbert, 1867).

18. *Honolulu Star-Bulletin*, September 30, 1929, 9. The text's subsequent quoted descriptions of the building and its landscape also derive from this source.

19. See Kenneth L. Ames, *On Bishop Street* (Honolulu: First Hawaiian Bank, 1996).

20. February 20, 1928, letter from Hart Wood to C. W. Dickey.

21. For information on the Henry Inn Apartments, see *Honolulu Advertiser*, August 9, 1931, 12, and September 13, 1931, 16.

22. *Honolulu Advertiser*, June 5, 1927, 13. Further discussion of the house can be found in the *Honolulu Advertiser* of May 9, 1926, 13, and *Architect and Engineer* (October 1929).

23. Letter, Hart Wood to Jesse Stanton, December 15, 1933.

24. Notable public buildings to appear during these two decades include the following: York and Sawyer's Federal Building in Honolulu; Louis Davis' Honolulu Police Station and McKinley High School; C. W. Dickey's Maui High School, Wailuku Library, and Territorial Office Building in Wailuku; Robert Miller's series of fire stations in Honolulu; William Desmond's Waialua Elementary School; Harry K. Stewart's Baldwin High School on Maui and Territorial Tax Office in Honolulu. In addition, the private sector contributed such noteworthy buildings as Julia Morgan's YWCA; York and Sawyer's Hawaiian Electric Building; Bertram Goodhue's Academy of Arts and Bank of Hawaii; Ralph Fishbourne's St. Patrick's Church; Warren and Wetmore's Royal Hawaiian Hotel; and David Adler's Dillingham residence, giving the passerby the impression that perhaps the 1917 recommendations of Goodhue and Mulgardt might actually become reality.

25. Original blueprints, Honolulu Hale, Sheets 24 and 25, found in the City and County Building Department.

26. *Honolulu Star-Bulletin*, June 29, 1929, 11, and July 6, 1929, 11.

Chapter 7: *The Depression Years and World War II*

1. June 27, 1932, letter from Hart Wood to Jesse Stanton; and July 8, 1932, letter from Hart Wood to J. S. Fairweather.

2. June 30, 1931, letters from Hart Wood to Kramer and Newman. In all likelihood,

Wood knew Newman through his associations with the Christian Science Church. Newman had come to Hawaii to design a church on Wilder Avenue for the Christian Scientists in 1917. Although the building was constructed, it was not used long by the church. The building was sold and became the Scottish Rites Masonic Temple, which still stands in Makiki. Wood's connection to Kramer most likely derives from one or both of the two major projects York and Sawyer undertook in Hawaii during the 1920s: the downtown post office and Hawaiian Electric Building.

3. June 12, 1931, and June 25, 1931, letters from Hart Wood to A. Livingston Gump of Consolidated Amusement.

4. The *Honolulu Advertiser* of June 17, 1934, 16, reported the following data on the decline in the value of building permits:

- 1929: 3,577 permits, for a total value of $7,254,042
- 1930: 2,042 permits, for a total value of $5,921,415
- 1931: 2,176 permits, for a total value of $3,622,440
- 1932: 2,128 permits, for a total value of $2,522,881
- 1933: 2,035 permits, for a total value of $1,408,302

5. *Honolulu Star-Bulletin*, June 11, 1932, 13.

6. *Honolulu Star-Bulletin*, February 19, 1929, 8.

7. These can still be witnessed in Hawaii in the Hana Courthouse and a few extant plantation workers' houses on Kauai.

8. *Garden Isle*, October 17, 1933, 1. A number of other issues of the *Garden Isle* also had front-page articles on the construction of this building. Some of the more pertinent include the following: April 11, 1933, 1; August 8, 1933, 1; August 29, 1933, 1; October 3, 1933, 1; and October 10, 1933, 1.

9. *California Arts and Architecture* 53 (April 1938): 29.

10. The Dr. William Wynn residence appears in the *Honolulu Advertiser*, April 5, 1925, 11. The Diamond Head Terrace houses were covered in the *Honolulu Advertiser*, April 13, 1924, 14, and the Princess Tract houses were mentioned in the *Honolulu Star-Bulletin*, April 21, 1920, 8.

11. See the *Honolulu Advertiser*, August 12, 1934, 14. In addition to Hart Wood being awarded the Ewa Plantation Administration Building, other commissions went to Ralph Fishbourne for the Ewa Hospital, William Furer for the Ewa Plantation Store, C. W. Dickey for the Waialua Hospital, and Mark Potter for the Waialua Administration Building.

12. *Honolulu Advertiser*, May 10, 1935, 9.

13. "Beauty in Utility," *Paradise of the Pacific* (February 1948): 20.

14. *Honolulu Advertiser*, August 8, 1937, 20, and August 22, 1937, 14.

15. C. W. Dickey, "New Atmosphere Is Seen in Modern Architecture," *Honolulu Star-Bulletin*, February 12, 1938, special section, 2.

16. Ray Morris, "Simplicity: New Trend in Home Design," *Honolulu Star-Bulletin*, February 12, 1938, special section, 5, and C. W. Conrad, "Sees Modern Tendencies in Island Homes," *Honolulu Star-Bulletin*, February 12, 1938, special section, 7.

17. Hart Wood, "Architects Must Preserve Island Charm," *Honolulu Star-Bulletin*, February 12, 1938, special section, 5.

18. World's Fair observations were recorded in a 74-page document by Hart Wood entitled "Notes of the Trip" constituting daily logs from their departure on September 15, 1939 through December 13, 1939. They were in New York City from October 2 through October 23.

19. Hart Wood, "Hawaii People Appreciate Good Architecture," undated clipping.

20. July 28, 1950, letter from Wood to Col. Francis Faulkner, District Engineer at Fort Armstrong.

21. According to son Kenneth Wood, his mother had a breakdown shortly after they arrived in Hawaii. She apparently also recovered well enough to be remembered by some of Wood's employees in the late 1940s and early 1950s. However, Kenneth Wood said she spent much of the last part of her life confined in a home at 3144 Monsarrat Avenue, and that she didn't even know when Hart Wood died. She outlived her husband, dying at the age of seventy-nine in November of 1960. Information on the death of Lt. Thomas Wood appears in the *Honolulu Star-Bulletin*, September 11, 1944, 7.

Chapter 8: *Reopening His Office*

1. January 8, 1947, letter from William Burgett to Hart Wood.

2. Article, "Battle Royal Rages Over Court Building," *Honolulu Advertiser*, February 23, 1940, 1; letter to the editor by Hart Wood, *Honolulu Advertiser*, February 24, 1940. In the article, Wood is quoted as making specific criticisms about the lack of ventilation, poor natural light, and the placement of rooms. In the subsequent letter to the editor, Wood minces no words in his critique of other recently completed buildings. Among other things, he says, "The present political system is responsible for the notorious Territorial Office building and several other public buildings, more or less equally ugly, if not so well publicized, and for not a single one that I can think of that is of any architectural or esthetic merit."

3. October 7, 1946, letter to Roger Benezet.

4. December 16, 1946, letter to William Burgett. Burgett was offered $350 per month plus a share of the profits.

5. January 8, 1947, letter from William Burgett to Hart Wood.

6. June 1947 letter to Cole McFarland in Washington, D.C., from Hart Wood.

7. Letter dated October 6, 1947, to Lyman Bigelow from Hart Wood.

8. Letter from Wood to Colonel B. M. Harloe, Department of the Army, May 5, 1949. Weed is listed as an associate; John Lau, Paul Anthopoulos, and Doug Yanagihara as senior drafters; Noboru Inouye as a junior drafter; and Maxine McQueen as the secretary. Weed probably joined Wood in late 1948. Weed's resume shows he was registered as an architect in New Jersey in 1934 and that he was registered as a structural and mechanical engineer in 1935. He became registered in Hawaii in 1947. Weed was listed in the 1947–1948 City Directory as the manager of the Honolulu Planing Mill. In 1949 he was listed as an architect working at Wood's residence. His only architectural experience listed

on his resume was from before he became registered in New Jersey. His experience from 1932 on was primarily as an engineer on various projects. His degree is from Princeton, where he got an MFA. He obtained a structural engineering degree from the Trenton Arts and Industrial School in 1934.

9. Letter from Wood to Jesse Stanton, December 13, 1948. Stanton was an architect in San Francisco whom Wood worked with first in 1927, while Stanton was at Gladding McBean during the time the work for the A and B Building was being done.

10. Douglas Yanagihara remembered working on this project while in the office from 1947 to late 1949.

11. Douglas Yanagihara said in an interview that Wood did a lot of design in charcoal. He gave a lot of responsibility away in the residential designs, primarily playing the role of reviewer. Yanagihara remembers Wood spending an entire week just designing new grillwork for Alexander & Baldwin near the ramp and that he was very finicky about this. Noboru Inouye was an apprentice at Hart Wood's office from 1948 through 1952. He remembers that Wood was active most of the time there. Inouye commented that Wood did freehand sketches and was a "very quiet man."

12. Letter from Wood to Colonel B. M. Harloe, Department of the Army, May 5, 1949.

13. In an application for work with the Hawaii Housing Authority dated November 7, 1949, Wood lists himself, Weed, John Lau, Noboru Inouye, and secretary Jane Kiyabu on staff.

14. In a letter from Wood to Jesse Stanton dated August 11, 1949, Wood says, "Jobs under construction are drying up for lack of materials some of which are on the ship strike bound in the harbor and new jobs are languishing because of the uncertainty of the future."

15. Several letters to and from leasing companies in March, April, and May of 1950 in Hart Wood's correspondence files.

16. The original drawings of the Lihue Union Church are dated October 5, 1950, under the firm name of "Hart Wood and E. A. Weed Associates."

17. Four tracings drawn by John Lau, Noboru Inouye, and Ed Weed, dated September 5, 1950. The house was in Kailua.

Chapter 9: *The Crepuscular Years, the End of a Career*

1. Patty Wood interview: She married Hart Dewitt Wood in 1956. Mrs. Wood died two years later. She thought Hart Sr. had Parkinson's disease. She mentioned he broke his hip in a fall at Maunalani. Hart Sr. was very difficult. Everything had to be perfect. He was not active for the last five years. "He always designed everything." For Mrs. Alice Spaulding Bowen, if anything was broken he would come down and make sure it got fixed. The last job she knows he had a lot to do with was the Kalanianaole Pumping Station, just opposite Summer Street. They gave him a ride to see it. He had Bob and Catherine Thompson do most of his landscaping.

2. "Conversion of Building 53 for Emergency Mine Assembly, West Loch, U.S.

Naval Ammunition Depot," drawing dated October 3, 1952, Hart Wood and E. A. Weed Architects, Drawn by J. A., checked by H. W. This was an open-sided, wood-framed extension to an existing building about eighty-four feet long and forty feet wide.

3. For example, in an Ormand Kelly interview on December 8, 1997, Kelly said he came to Hawaii to work with Wood, Weed, and Kubala in 1959. Ed Kubala was already gone. Wallace was around but left shortly thereafter. Ormand was the architect of record. Weed was not living in Hawaii at that time and came down from New York to consult before getting tired of making the trip. Ed Weed was ten to fifteen years Ormand's senior. He said Weed was specification oriented, not design oriented. He thinks Weed ended up in Darian, Connecticut.

4. *Honolulu Advertiser*, May 16, 1954.

INDEX

271

ABOUT THE AUTHORS

With careers of mirrored and interactive interests, the authors of the work have many years of combined experience in the fields of architecture, architectural history, and historic preservation. Don J. Hibbard, Ph.D., administered the State of Hawaii's historic preservation program from 1981 to 2002 and now works as a heritage specialist. He has written several books on the Islands' architecture, including *The View from Diamond Head* and *Designing Paradise*. Glenn Mason, AIA, heads his own architectural firm, Mason Architects, in Honolulu and has published a number of articles and essays on Hawaii's historic architecture. Born and raised in Hawaii, he has practiced architecture in the Islands for more than thirty years. Karen J. Weitze, Ph.D., is an architectural historian living in California who has worked on historic preservation projects across the nation, including Hawaii and the Pacific. She is the author of *California's Mission Revival* and a primary contributor to *The Arts and Crafts Movement in California: Living the Good Life.*

Production notes for Hibbard / *Hart Wood*

Jacket and interior design by Julie Matsuo-Chun

Display type in Perpetua Titling MT; text in Arno Pro

Printing and binding by Thomson-Shore, Inc.

Printed on 70# Huron Matte, 540 ppi